D0990774

Twayne's English Authors Series

Sylvia E. Bowman, *Editor*

INDIANA UNIVERSITY

Richard Lovelace

TEAS 96

Richard Lovelace

By MANFRED WEIDHORN

Yeshiva University

Twayne Publishers, Inc. :: New York

821
L89zw

Copyright © 1970 by Twayne Publishers, Inc.

All Rights Reserved

Library of Congress Catalog Card Number: 70–99542

MANUFACTURED IN THE UNITED STATES OF AMERICA

DEDICATION

To my Mother and Ben
And to the Memory of my Father, Aron

APR 6 '71]

HUNT LIBRARY
CARNEGIE-MELLON UNIVERSITY

Preface

The name Richard Lovelace is known to even the casual reader, two or three of his poems appear in every anthology of great English literature, and his lines, "Stone walls do not a prison make," "I could not love thee, dear, so much,/Lov'd I not Honour more," have become as proverbial as any by Shakespeare. Yet most of his work is read by very few, studied by fewer. One small and severely circumscribed book and a few scattered essays are all that have been devoted to him—in a century which has given renewed, close attention to his contemporaries. This study is, therefore, an attempt to remedy the situation.

Making no pretense that Lovelace is an undiscovered giant, a neglected genius at last deserving of a "revival," this study examines his poetry, separates the considerable portion that is good from the equally sizable amount that is hopelessly bad, and attempts an interpretation. The focus is inevitably on the better pieces, and the rest of his work is used only as it sheds light on the famous, perfect lyrics. Viewed sympathetically, Lovelace's poetry, though only occasionally reaching the heights, has its charms and insights.

After an introduction which sketches the little that is known of the poet's life, five chapters are devoted to the themes of his poetry. Chapter 7 studies his imagery; Chapter 8 considers prosody, syntax, and over-all organization. After assaying the influences, Classical and Donnean, on Lovelace and his possible influence on others, the book concludes with a sketch of his reputation through the ages and with a final evaluation of his work.

Because not much has been written on Lovelace, the bibliography, while selective, includes every sizable article and leaves out only dated material or brief notes. These may, in any case, be found in the footnotes at the appropriate places. The standard edition of Lovelace's poems is by C. H. Wilkinson (Oxford University Press, 1930). Throughout this study, however, I shall be quoting from the 1931 edition of R. G. Howarth in the Everyman Library series. The latter text, equally complete, has the advantages of being readily available and of modernizing spelling and punctuation without altering the meaning. Page and line numbers after each quotation refer to this book.

Grateful acknowledgment is made to E. P. Dutton & Co., Inc. for permission to quote from the poems of Richard Lovelace as they appear in the Everyman's Library Edition of *Minor Poets of the Seventeenth Century* edited by R. G. Howarth.

MANFRED WEIDHORN

Yeshiva University
New York City

Contents

Chronology

1618   Richard Lovelace born, either in Woolwich, Kent, or in Holland.

1629   King Charles I nominates "Thomas [probably Richard] Lovelace," upon petition of Lovelace's mother, Anne Barne Lovelace, to Sutton's foundation at Charterhouse.

1631   On May 5, Lovelace is made "Gentleman Wayter Extraordinary" to the king.

1634   On June 27, he matriculates as Gentleman Commoner at Gloucester Hall, Oxford.

1635   Writes a comedy, *The Scholars*.

1636   On August 31, the degree of M.A. is conferred on him. ("The Vintage to the Dungeon"?)

1637   On October 4, he enters Cambridge University.

1638   Lovelace returns to the court of Charles I.

1638– His first printed poems appear: "An Elegy" on Princess
1639   Katherine; prefaces to several books.

1639   He is senior ensign in General Goring's regiment in the First Scottish Expedition. "Sonnet to Goring." ("To Lucasta, going to the Wars"?)

1640   Commissioned captain in the Second Scottish Expedition; writes a tragedy, *The Soldier*. Returning home to Kent, he enters at twenty-one into the possession of his family property.

1641   Lovelace tears up a pro-Parliament, anti-Episcopacy petition at a meeting in Maidstone, Kent.

1642   On April 30, he presents the anti-Parliamentary Petition of Kent and is imprisoned at Gatehouse. After appealing, he is released on bail, June 21. Civil War begins August 22. ("To Althea, from Prison," "To Lucasta. From Prison"?) In September he goes to Holland with General Goring. ("To Lucasta, going beyond the Seas," "The Rose"?)

1642– Probably serves in Holland and France with General
1646   Goring. "The Scrutiny."

1643   Sells some of his property to Richard Hulse.

1644   Death of brother William at Carmarthen, Wales, under
the command of another brother, Colonel Francis.

1646   In October, he is wounded at Dunkirk while fighting under
the Great Condé against the Spaniards.

1647   On October 26, he is admitted to the Freedom of the
Painters' Company.

1648   On February 4, *Lucasta* is licensed at the Stationer's Register. On June 9, Lovelace is again imprisoned (at Peterhouse).

1649   On April 9, Lovelace is released; sells the remaining family
property and portraits to Richard Hulse again. On May
14, *Lucasta* is published.

1650– Lovelace's whereabouts and fortune unknown, although
1657   various poems are written.

1657   Lovelace dies (circumstances unknown).

1659– *Lucasta. Posthume Poems* is published.
1660

Richard Lovelace

HUNT LIBRARY
CARNEGIE-MELLON UNIVERSITY

CHAPTER 1

"Of Mars and Minerva": Life and Works

I *The Cavalier*

RICHARD LOVELACE was born in 1618, either in Woolwich, Kent, or in Holland, of old Kentish stock. Related to the Lovelaces of Canterbury and of Hurley (Berkshire), the family held property at Bethersden, Chart, Halden, Shadoxhurst, and Canterbury from 1368 until 1649, when Lovelace himself had to sell everything in the wake of Royalist defeat. His grandfather and father, both named Sir William, were professional soldiers. The grandfather, one of those knighted by the Earl of Essex during his notorious 1599 Irish expedition, accumulated considerable holdings; the father, given a license in 1604 to serve any Christian state in league with England, attained the rank of colonel in the States General Army in 1607. Knighted in 1609 by James I, he married Anne Barne.

The bride's family was close to the legal profession, her grandfather having been Chief Baron of the Exchequer under Elizabeth. The couple settled in her native town, Woolwich, but made several trips to Holland, on one of which the poet may have been born. Of their eight children, Richard was the oldest. One of his four brothers, Francis, became a colonel in the Civil War and, in 1668, governor of the New York colony recently wrested from the Dutch.

The father, a man "of great courage," was killed at the siege of Groll in 1627 at the age of forty-four, when Richard was but nine. His widow remarried three years later. In 1629, while still single, she petitioned Charles I for the nomination of one of her sons to Sutton's Hospital Foundation—a "scholarship," in our terms—at the Charterhouse school in London. This petition was a common one among great families who were financially embarrassed. The king nominated "Thomas Lovelace," but most scholars consider this entry a scribe's mistake for "Richard," the only one of the sons old enough to qualify. After the birth of a daughter, the mother died, leaving her husband and her brother guardians of her children.

Since there is no record of any Lovelace at Charterhouse, C. H. Wilkinson conjectures that, the recent death of the grandfather having placed the youth beyond the need of financial assistance, Richard attended school as a "boarder"—as a scion of higher social position than was a "scholar." [1] Lovelace must have been at Charterhouse for five years, three of them with Richard Crashaw, who developed into a poet of entirely different sensibility.

On May 5, 1631, Lovelace was sworn in as a "Gentleman Wayter Extraordinary" to the King, an honorary position for which one paid a fee and which he still held in 1641. This was his formal introduction to the court milieu where he later flourished, but first came further polishing at Oxford University. On June 27, 1634, Lovelace matriculated as Gentleman Commoner at Gloucester Hall (afterwards Gloucester, now Worcester, College); his stepfather, Dr. Jonathan Browne, had been a member of the Hall. Lovelace was then, as Anthony à Wood put it, "accounted the most amiable and beautiful person that ever eye beheld, a person also of innate modesty, virtue and courtly deportment, which made him then, but especially after, when he retired to the great city, much admired and adored by the female sex." [2]

During his first year at Oxford, he wrote a comedy, *The Scholars*. As a result of the king's interest in drama and masque, amateur playwriting proliferated in the 1630's among courtiers, university wits, and Inns of Court men. Performed first at Gloucester Hall and later "acted with applause" at the Whitefriars, Salisbury Court, *The Scholars* was never printed.

In the late summer of 1636, a three-week celebration was held at Oxford, attended by Charles I, as well as William Laud, Chancellor of the University and Archbishop of Canterbury. During the festivities, on August 31, Lovelace, among such prominent companions as Prince Rupert, Charles's nephew, was granted the Master of Arts degree. This "signal honour" for one barely eighteen and only two years at the university was conferred, according to Wood, at the solicitation of a "great lady belonging to the queen." But as gentleman waiter to the king, Lovelace had sufficient standing at court to receive the degree without the help of any ladies.

On October 4, 1637, Lovelace was enrolled into Cambridge

University. There he remained a few months, becoming acquainted with such men as Andrew Marvell, who were to write commendatory verses to the *Lucasta* volume a decade later. In 1638, Lovelace came in "great splendour" to the court of Charles I, "the most cultivated Court [England] has ever known." Under Charles, royal patronage of the arts in England reached its apex, only to end abruptly with the Civil War. As Margaret Pickel describes it, "Never since . . . has there been an English Court which was a center of literary life, or a body of Court poetry which bore the mark of a personal devotion to the King as patron." It was, in fact, the last Renaissance court in England.[3]

The climate there, vividly reflected in Thomas Carew's poetry and Anthony Van Dyck's paintings, was one of "a dignified voluptuousness, an exquisite elegance." Under the well-read, intelligent, demure king, a sobriety and refinement, a moral decorum, replaced some of the more uninhibited behavior of the previous two reigns. The king, a connoisseur of literature, drama, and the arts, surrounded himself with and enjoyed the esteem of talented people of like interest. He was a patron of the painters Van Dyck, Rubens, Peter Lely; the musician Henry Lawes; the poets Ben Jonson, William Davenant, Thomas Carew, John Suckling, Abraham Cowley, Edmund Waller; and of a host of lesser figures. Remote from the people and from political realities, the court fostered a coterie atmosphere, a certain frivolity; as political disaster approached, the poets spent their time imploring Amarantha to unravel her hair. The French queen, Henrietta Maria, brought with her a dignified, rather superficial ambiance, a primness expressed in the fad for "platonic love" and in the *Précieuse* aim to refine manners and speech, especially in relations between the sexes.

At Whitehall, Lovelace became acquainted with other courtier-poets, including Carew, the "oracle of love," and Suckling, the gayest of versifiers. Suckling's famous "Ballad of a Wedding" may indeed be addressed to Lovelace: "I tell thee, Dick. . . ." Such a milieu encouraged the writing of poetry, which had in any case been an accomplishment of well-bred English gentlemen since the time of Thomas Wyatt and the Earl of Surrey at the court of Henry VIII.

No mere scribbler, Lovelace achieved some eminence as a poet. When the Princess Katherine died on the day of her birth, he was sought out two years after leaving Oxford for a contribution (his first printed poem) to a volume of elegies by Oxford men. His prefatory lines years later for John Hall's translation of Hierocles and for John Fletcher's *Wild Goose Chase* were given the place of honor. His poems were solicited, quickly set to music by the leading composers of the time; he was in demand as a patron; he had become a presence at the university and at court. As A. E. Waite indicates, Lovelace's talents might have taken him far if he had had room for development; instead, with events at home rapidly coming to a crisis, he was thrown into a stormy time and wasted the "splendors of his intellect and the resources of his inheritance" in the political struggles.[4] Poetry writing was ultimately ancillary to the vocations of soldier and courtier.

England was rent by the growing struggle between established church and Puritan reformers, between king and Parliament. The years of debate and exhortation were replaced by days of violence and the gathering of forces. The courtiers responded with élan to Charles's call to lead the king's army. They were, for the most part, men of dash and adventure who followed their leader rather than ideologists concerned with the religious and political principles at issue. Such Cavaliers saw in their own brief careers the coup de grâce administered by Parliament and Puritan to the dying romantic dream of chivalry.

Accepted as a soldier by George, Lord Goring, later Earl of Norwich, Lovelace served in the regiment of Goring's son, General George Goring, in the Bishops' wars of 1639–40. Lovelace's senior by ten years, General Goring had had experience in the Dutch wars and was another of the dashing, talented, intriguing, spendthrift young men about the court. Lovelace was senior ensign in the first Scottish expedition of 1639, and captain in the second of 1640.

There was nothing romantic about these two ventures. When the ill-equipped English forces were subject to the rigors of the weather and were confronted with twenty thousand Scots and veterans, Charles I turned to negotiations and, in order to gain time, signed the Pacification of Berwick on June 18, 1639. Frustrated by inglorious reality—"now that the peace is made at the foe's rate"—Lovelace turned inwards, in a mood of poetic whimsy, for the heroic ideal. The "Sonnet to Goring," Lovelace's only reference to the Scottish wars, is a piece of bravado, of factitious bacchanalian exuberance which lavishes praise on Goring's charms and on his bride's beauty amid the paucity of martial exploits to celebrate.

Eventually rejecting the treaty, Charles undertook the following year a second expedition. That proved a worse disaster than the first; and, in the Treaty of Ripon of October 26, 1640, he yielded Northumberland and Durham. At about this time, Lovelace wrote a tragedy, *The Soldier*. The title indicates that this play, like the earlier, was based on recent experiences; and the change of genre from comedy to tragedy is suggestive. Such a play may well have contained reflections on the dispiriting way things were turning out, may have dramatized the cavalier in duress as he confronted the dissipation of his idea of himself. How different, after all, had court and camp turned out to be from the innocence and promise at the university! All this is conjecture, to be sure; the playhouses were soon to close, and the text of this play, like its predecessor, has not survived.

Lovelace returned from Scotland in his majority. Doffing his war gear, he went home to Kent to enter into the possession of his lands and to assume the privileges and duties—such as Justice of the Peace—of a country gentleman. Some of the Lovelace property was gone by now; what remained gave him a sufficient but modest annual income of five hundred pounds. At this time in Parliament, moderate men like Hyde and Falkland, while initially with the reformers, began to sympathize with the king and desired to end the harassment of royal power. Thus Sir Edward Deering, though no friend of the church, drew up a petition to reinstitute the liturgy, retain Episcopacy, and restore the king to his rights. This petition angered Parliament and caused the drawing up of counterpetitions. In Maidstone, Kent, one such counterpetition was being drafted after debate. Suddenly a group—led by Lovelace, who was in attendance as justice of the peace—clapped on its hats in an act of disrespect, seized the petition, tore it up, and strewed it on the floor.

Soon thereafter, in 1642, Lovelace was chosen, perhaps as a result of his defiant act, to deliver personally, with an attendant on Charles I (Sir William Boteler), to the House of Commons Deering's petition, on behalf of the county of Kent. One of the men who signed the document, however, changed his mind and warned the authorities. The House was consequently prepared for trouble when Lovelace appeared on April 30, 1642, with some followers. The petition was read and, as Lovelace and Boteler withdrew, debated. When a Captain Leigh related Lovelace's behavior at Maidstone, Lovelace was called and questioned. Answering everything with candor, he asserted that the disclaiming anti-Royalist petition he had shredded at Maidstone had already been disavowed by all the justices there.

Unconvinced, the House sent Lovelace to the Gatehouse prison in Westminster, while dismissing the rest with a reprimand. Charges against Lovelace were prepared, but nothing came of them. Bail was fixed in June, upon Lovelace's petition for release. This request to the House is, in effect, the only extant piece of prose from the hand of Lovelace; and C. H. Hartmann describes it as filled with "tactful and insinuating flattery and yet in no way expressing any penitence for the offence." [5] Having been in prison seven weeks and being "full of submission," Lovelace asked for freedom in order to serve in Ireland against the rebels. The House released Lovelace, June 21, on bail. Though the charges against him were dropped, he remained a man under suspicion; he was forbidden to have anything to do with the army or even to leave London without permission. Thus was he disabled at a critical juncture: just two months later, the civil war began in earnest.

Waite considers the presentation of the Kentish petition the turning point of Lovelace's life. It is indeed true that his already shaky family fortunes went into a long decline thereafter, together with those of the English monarchy he supported. At the same time, such a disaster may have had its redeeming side if it was responsible, as many scholars believe, for the creation of one of the finest lyrics in English, "To Althea, From Prison."

Lovelace's whereabouts after his release are uncertain. Prohibited from personally aiding the king's cause, he sold most of his lands in 1643 and used the money, according to Wood,

either to keep up the credit and reputation of the king's cause by furnishing men with horse and arms, or by relieving ingenious men in want, whether scholars, musicians, soldiers, etc. Also by furnishing his two brothers, Colonel Francis Lovelace and Captain William Lovelace . . . with men and money for the king's cause, and his other brother called Dudley Posthumus Lovelace with moneys for his maintenance in Holland to study tactics and fortification in that school of war.

Wilkinson conjectures that Lovelace spent the greater part of 1643–46 in Holland and France, with return trips to England for affairs of business in March, 1643, and in August, 1645.[6] He may have visited Holland as early as September, 1642, in the train of his old chief, General Goring, who, after the surrender of Portsmouth, left to recruit English troops among those in the Dutch service. Through Goring, Lovelace met Princess Louisa of Bohemia in Holland; he was also in Rotterdam. Quotations from an untranslated Dutch writer in one of his poems indicate that he mastered the language. Verses by Andrew Marvell and by John Tatham to Lovelace in Holland, urging his return, referred to the many ladies, especially Althea, who missed him.

A different facet of Lovelace's character is evinced by such poems. During those years, the Fleece Tavern, off Covent Garden, was the meeting place of a group of minor poets and wits led by Sir Aston Cockain and Charles Cotton the elder, and including Francis Lenton, Edward Sherburne, Thomas Stanley, John Tatham, Henry Glapthorne, William Hammond, and John Hall. Though intellectual interests must have been their common bond, some of them later addressed poems to Lovelace rife with military imagery; Lovelace apparently saw himself as, above all, a soldier. A sizable number of the commendatory poems for Lovelace's first volume were written by soldiers, many of them holding the rank of colonel. As eldest son in a family with a long line of warriors, Lovelace was a Cavalier to his very marrow.

The main soldiering in the Civil War at home, however, was done by his brothers. Reports of a "Col. Lovelace" at Carmarthen in 1644–45 refer to his brother Francis, who governed the town and surrendered it after a seesaw battle in October, 1646. His brother William, who served under Francis's command, died in battle there in 1644. Other reports of a "Captain Lovelace" are about the youngest brother, Dudley. Lovelace himself served with the French under the Great Condé against the Spaniards in Holland and was wounded at Dunkirk in October, 1646. So the Kentish country gentleman had become a soldier of fortune abroad, following in the footsteps of his father and grandfather in an earlier, and happier, age.

Yet another aspect of Lovelace is manifested by his being admitted on October 26, 1647, along with the painter Peter Lely, to the Freedom of the Painters' Company. An immigrant from Hol-

land, Lely had succeeded Van Dyck as the English court painter.
When Charles I was kidnapped and confined, Lely painted him
with his second son, the Duke of York. Lovelace celebrated both
subject and painter in a poem expressing loyalty to king and lauding Lely's genius. It was Lely too who later designed the plates
for Lovelace's two books of poems, including the engraving of
Lucasta. Lovelace had, clearly, become an important gentleman
of taste, well known to painters. One of his close friends and the
subject of several of his poems was Endymion Porter, principal
artistic consultant and purchasing agent for Charles I, himself one
of the few in England with any appreciation of Renaissance painting. Lovelace's exile in Holland, we should also remember, was
during the Golden Age of the Dutch School, when Rembrandt
was almost forty.

Lovelace seems always to have been surrounded by what we
would now consider an intellectual circle. A distant cousin,
Thomas Stanley, and a great uncle, George Sandys, were poets
and translators. His intimate friends included Lely, Porter,
Charles Cotton the elder and the younger, as well as Marvell and
various composers and painters. Through Stanley and Sherburne,
as well as through his own limited travels, he became acquainted
with late Renaissance poetry in France, Italy, and Spain. A sign of
a generosity of spirit is that after the outbreak of hostilities, he
wrote a highly laudatory poem to John Hall and was himself the
subject of high praise in prefatory lines written by Hall and by
Andrew Marvell for the 1649 Lucasta; both Hall and Marvell
were among the few poets committed to the Parliamentary side. A
newssheet even attacked Hall for consorting with such as Lovelace, but political differences were not allowed to shatter friend-
ships in the republic of letters.

In the flower of his career, Lovelace must at this time have sat
for the painting hanging in the Dulwich Collection; and it, with
the Hollar engraving in Lucasta, is the only extant known portrait
of the poet. Depicting the ideal cultured soldier and poet, a cavalier in the best sense, it radiates an air of Castiglione's sprezzatura
("careless disdain") and accords with Aubrey's description of
Lovelace as "a most beautiful gentleman . . . one of the hand-
somest men in England . . . extraordinarily handsome Man, but
proud." Here is, Philip Lindsay discerningly comments, no cynic's
face like Suckling's, no visionary like George Herbert, no voluptu-

ary like Carew. Instead, the portrait reveals a sensitive, melancholy, courageous demeanor, hurt by life, questioning its secrets, yet unafraid, secure, even almost haughty.[7] "The courtier's, scholar's, soldier's eye, tongue, sword."

And then Lovelace's world fell apart. In April, 1648, a series of risings occurred on behalf of Charles I. At Maidstone, the Parliamentary forces under Lord Fairfax—who was served and poetically lauded by Marvell—prevailed. Their troops came to Lovelace's house in search of his brother Francis. As they seized a cabinet of jewels, Lovelace protested. He was thereupon committed to prison a second time (this time at Peterhouse) on the pretext that his papers were not in order.

He did not receive the leniency given the other prisoners. Either because of actual connection with Royalist agitation in Kent or as a precautionary step taken in time of trouble and on the basis of his earlier activities (and with three brothers devoted to the cause), Lovelace remained in prison for six months. He spent his time in preparing his poems for the press. As A. E. Waite says, "forced to lay aside his sword . . . [he] sought in the creations of a poetic mind, relief from the monotony of prison life, from sorrow for his king's misfortunes, and doubtless, too, from many dark thoughts about his own future." [8] His brother Dudley had been apprehended in June, 1648, while brother Francis continued fighting until the surrender of the king's army on August 28, 1648, just six years after the start of the war.

A petition for release of Lovelace was denied in October, 1648. December of that year saw Pride's Purge of Commons; and, when Lovelace was finally released, on April 10, 1649, he stepped into a commonwealth ruled by Puritans and generals. Charles I had been tried and executed; the ominous Oliver Cromwell was in the ascendant. The Royalist had now to make themselves inconspicuous. Thus, at the age of thirty-one and in this bleak hour, Lovelace disappears from view: nothing is known of the remaining decade of his life.

The prospect must have seemed as dour for Lovelace and his family as for his cause and country. In 1643 he had sold some of the family land to one Richard Hulse. Now he sold to the same man all the remaining property, including the family seat at Bethersden and the family portraits left by his mother. (The portraits eventually came into the possession of Dulwich College in 1687, where seven of the eight may still be seen.) The one bright spot in this dark year was the appearance on May 14 of *Lucasta:/Epodes, Odes, Sonnets,/Songs, &c./to Which Is Added/Aramantha,/A Pastorall./By/Richard Lovelace,/Esq.* Yet even this event may not have been too auspicious: for gentlemen to publish their poetry was indecorous. It is possible that Lovelace, in serious financial straits, needed any money he could obtain by capitalizing on the fame that such lyrics as "To Althea, From Prison" and "The Scrutiny" had achieved. Thus the collection and publication of his poetry was probably brought about by two adversities— tedium while in prison; penury when outside it. The book had been licensed at the Stationer's Register on February 4 of the previous year; and Lovelace had put his incarceration to good use, for Wilkinson has found many signs of revision, some even made while the book was in press.

A decade later appeared *Lucasta./Posthume Poems.* The poet may well have been himself preparing the second volume for the press at the time of his death. Though dated 1659, the book appeared in 1660, edited by Dudley and by Eldred Revett. Together with *Elegies Sacred to the Memory of the Author: By Several of his Friends,* it contained portraits of Lovelace and Althea. Not many copies were printed of either the 1649 or 1659 volumes, nor did they sell very quickly. Only thirty-one copies of the earlier and nine of the later survive.

Lovelace's death probably occurred in 1657. In a controverted passage, Wood said:

Having by that time consumed all his estate, [Lovelace] grew very melancholy (which brought him at length into a consumption), became very poor in body and purse, was the object of charity, went in ragged clothes . . . mostly lodged in obscure and dirty places, more befitting the worst of beggars, and poorest of servants. . . . He died in a very mean lodging in Gun-powder alley near Shoe-lane, and was buried at the west-end of the church of S. Bride alias Bridget in London, near the body of his kinsman.

Waite thinks that this picture of Lovelace's poverty is probably an exaggeration stemming from Lovelace's sale of all his property; Wilkinson discredits the story altogether, for none of the 1659 elegies on Lovelace makes reference to any unusual death.

But even if hyperbolic, the story dramatizes the severe decline in fortune after the brilliant beginning. "Thus early and tragically," Waite describes it, "closed a life which had opened with fairest promise, and which, by comparison with its morning splendours, could have been hardly endurable at the end." Whatever his end and however we choose to appraise the quality of his poetry, the life and style of the man was what impressed everyone, then and ever since. The elegies develop a theme already expressed in the commendatory poems of 1649—his prowess in both soldiering and poetry. They speak of a "double glory," a "Delphic wreath and civic coronet," Mars's banner and Minerva's bays. "Excellent in Arms, and Arts/ . . . few men of fame but knew/ He was tam Marti, quam Mercurio." Wood found Lovelace "eminent for his valor and poetry," "accounted by all those that well knew him, to have been a person well vers'd in the Greek and Latin poets, in music, whether practical or theoretical, instrumental or vocal, and in other things befitting a gentleman. Some of the said persons have also added in my hearing, that his common discourse was not only significant and witty, but incomparably graceful, which drew respect from all men and women." [9]

Where the elegies on Carew and Suckling refer to their "wittie" qualities, those on Lovelace praise his beauty of soul, his honour. Though his fate was like Suckling's, Lovelace stood for ideals which Suckling only faintly represented. More than the others, Lovelace was the paragon of the Renaissance gentleman, of the Cavalier, in a manner reminiscent of Sir Philip Sidney and Sir Walter Raleigh. Modern writers like Lindsay and C. V. Wedgwood remind us that, contemporary poetic hyperbole notwithstanding, Lovelace scarcely drew a sword in the wars at home and that his poetic achievement is far beneath, say, Marvell's. True enough; what he did or wrote is not so striking as what he was and stood for. His career was most representative of the tragedy of his era, perfectly expressed by his few great lyrics. He is one of the most romantic figures in English history and literature, the best known "Cavalier poet," the beau ideal, the graceful amateur who left behind him two slim volumes of verse not reprinted for one hundred and fifty years and an unforgettable portrait of a man. Lindsay sees him as one cheated by life—forced to be a father to his brothers and sisters from his youth, a soldier before he was a man, a lover without a wife or scion—a man who yet lived life to the full, remained true to everyone, receded into the dark a perfect cavalier "singing sweetly in the midst of the world's chaos and fearless of anyone or anything, save of dishonor." [10]

The epithet most frequently applied to Lovelace, "Cavalier," was used by him only once and that pejoratively. Originally referring, like "chivalry," to a horseman, horse-soldier, knight, it came to mean in Lovelace's time those who fought on the king's side; it was often a reproach hurled upon the Royalist swashbucklers who hailed the prospect of war. But the word has since come to stand for a whole way of life celebrated by Castiglione and symbolized by his concept of *sprezzatura:* for what is gallant, "brave" (in both modern and older senses), fine; for grace of deportment and love of beauty; for a gaiety and intimacy, simplicity and robustness; for the training of the courtly gentleman in arms and letters; and, by extension, for a careless manner. The Cavalier can do all things effortlessly, with slight involvement, as though the action were natural, not studied. Treating each accomplishment as a means or diversion only, he distrusts the overearnest, intense, specialized, professional. He uses a "recklessness to cover art." His is the stance, in our own vocabulary, of the "cool," of detachment amid involvement.

Nobleman trained in the arts and Classical languages, manifesting social polish and physical prowess; "university wit" who is also able to pay court in the most genteel manner to high-born ladies; a man equally at ease in fingering a sword or a recorder, a diplomatic note or a woman's breast; a man enjoying life to the fullest but ready to lay it down with a flourish for God, king, or love, at the drop of a petition or wink of a lady's eye; a man not troubled with the self-examination and complex feelings of the Elizabethan nobleman or the dandy depicted in Donne's love lyrics; a man more worldly and polished, if less intense and conscientious; a man, in short, who is the poetic and perhaps more bluff English version of Castiglione's Renaissance courtier (Castiglione, that is, modified by the Three Musketeers and Don Juan)—a Cavalier is thus a later, indeed a final, version of the Renaissance gentleman, Lovelace standing to Charles I as Sir Philip Sidney and Sir Walter Raleigh stood to Elizabeth I. Lovelace's is the last English generation brought up under the influence of the Italian Renaissance ideal. Courtier, landholder, man of affairs, soldier, scholar, connoisseur of painting, musician, wit, lover, he turned to poetry as but one accomplishment conferring additional honor, as "recreation for vacant hours."

At the same time, though carrying on the nobility of Sidney and Spenser, the generation of Lovelace and Suckling exhibits more the graces than grace; the chivalric stance without the corresponding soul; the gay colors covering a growing hollowness; a dilettantism instead of well-roundedness. The Neo-Platonism which for Spenser was a way of comprehending reality becomes now artificial and ornamental, a fashion in polite society. Gone too is the Christian commitment, the plumbing of the soul's depth. The poet no more wrestles with his destiny in this or the next life than he struggles with his verses. Without aspirations for composing comprehensive works, he writes between living experiences; but, treating his poetry as well as his life cavalierly, he does not bother to set down or explore all that he sees and feels. His curiosity and his horizon are limited. Like a last bloom of nobility, this Cavalier generation stands between the serious Elizabethan chivalry and the wittiness, buffoonery, and debauchery of the Rochester circle at the court of Charles II at a time when the all-embracing vision was to be entertained by someone outside, indeed opposed to, the court.

When on March 27, 1639, the anniversary of Charles I's coronation, the army, including in its ranks the handsome, poetic Lovelace and the extravagant Suckling, left on the First Scottish Expedition from which it would return in disarray and frustration, it took with it the end of an era. The court circle was quickly broken by war, flight, death; and the departure of the royal couple from Whitehall in 1642 was but the death knell. "In debts, defeat and hunger their voices fade out."

II *Who Is Lucasta? What Is She?*

It had long been a tradition for poets to celebrate in a series of lyrics their lady love, whose identity was hidden by a pseudonym. Catullus had his Lesbia; Propertius, his Cynthia; and, with the rise of sonnet cycles, Dante, his Beatrice; Petrarch, his Laura. The extent to which these quasi-fictional situations in the poetry were based on actual incident or were mere reveries and idealizations is uncertain. During the later Renaissance, sequences of hundreds of sonnets were written in Italy, France, and England devoted to a lady. Sometimes, the lover appears within the poems, also with a pseudonym—Sidney's Astrophel to Penelope Rich's Stella. The pseudonyms are usually neologisms with allegorical overtones or in some other way unlike the names people were likely to have in contemporary life.

In the seventeenth century, when the amatory sonnet tradition had ebbed, poets continued the convention of devoting most of their love lyrics to one pseudonymous lady, whose name occasionally adorned the title of the collection of their poems: Carew and Celia, Waller and Sacharissa, Habington and Castara. Robert Herrick, on the other hand, referred to nearly dozens of such ladies. Like Crashaw, he sometimes indicated that he was writing for a "supposed" mistress or wife; having a lady had become a cliché expected of poets. Lovelace falls between the two extremes: like Herrick, he uses several names; but, in the manner of the old tradition, he gives place of honor to "Lucasta." That name not only adorns the title of his two volumes but also appears in many of his poems.

Since the private, especially amatory, lives of poets are of interest to many readers, various attempts have been made to establish the identity of Lovelace's lady. Wood first set abroad a tale that took a long time to die: "He had made his amours to a gentlewoman of great beauty and fortune named Lucy Sacheverel, whom he usually called Lux Casta [chaste light]; but she upon a strong report that Lovelace was dead of his wound received at Dunkirk, soon after Married." The story probably rests on the enigmatic third line of the first stanza of "To Lucasta. From Prison," "Left for awhile another's bride" (264, 3).[11] This stanza says, in Wood's reading of it, that, since she forfeited the poet's devotion by marrying someone else in his absence, she should release him from his vows of love to her. While Hazlitt suggested that Althea was the one who became Lovelace's wife after Lucasta had married another, Waite challenged the notion that Lovelace subsequently married anyone.

Hartmann thinks that Lucasta is likely to be a real person if only because in the ode, "You are deceived," Lovelace mentions her alongside Habington's Castara and Waller's Sacharissa, both of whom were actual persons the poets courted and whose identity is known. To this view we might add further evidence. In the "Dialogue. Amyntor, Alexis," Alexis' deep love for Lucasta, "that bright Northern star," is said to prevent him from crossing the sea and joining his friend Amyntor. This poem is not a conventional love lyric but a "pastoral dialogue" with apparent personal references. In the manner of Sidney, Lovelace at times presented himself within the poetry under a pseudonym (Alexis). Amyntor, we know from other poems, is Lovelace's good friend Endymion Porter. Hence, we may assume that Lucasta is also real. Moreover, the following lines may contain a personal reference; they suggest that Lucasta came from a wealthy, middle-class family while he himself, as a member of the lower aristocracy, could offer her a name, rank, lands, a country manor:

> Ah, Lucasta, why so great
> That thy crammed coffers sweat!
> Yet not owner of a seat
> May shelter you from Nature's heat,
> And your earthly joys complete.
> (268, 10–14)

The matter of identification is complicated by the pastoral "Aramantha," the name of which—as if to further confound hope of solution—a critic has thought a misprint for Amarantha, a name in one of the lyrics. The heroine, happily living in rustic surroundings, runs by chance into her old lover, Alexis, from whom she has been separated for some time by what seems to be the Civil War. Her real name turns out to be Lucasta. As the poem ends, the two are said to live together happily forever after. Whether this poem is meant to be a representation of Lovelace and Miss X, and what exactly occurred—a betrothal perhaps, as Waite thinks—remains a mystery.[12]

Fictional or real, Lucasta is the inspiration of Lovelace's muse and appears in seventeen (1649) and ten (1659) poems. With one possible exception, all twenty-seven are Petrarchan, courtly poems, while the erotica prevails in poems addressed to the other ladies. This contrast suggests that there were two sides to Lovelace's thoughts on love, as there were to Dante's and Petrarch's. If we do not know who Lucasta is, the case with the other names is no better. But not all the ladies are likely to have been figments of the imagination; for, as we have noted, Lovelace was quite the philanderer.

The question of the ladies' identity is but part of the larger problem of the relation of the poetry to the poet's life. Lovelace seems to have been the sort of writer whose personal experiences are only sporadically and indirectly reflected in his work (if we omit the two missing plays). Little external and internal evidence exists for dating the poems. The better ones were probably written earlier in his career, in the years 1636–49. We cannot be sure, however, of many others; we do not even know if the body of the 1659 volume consists of verse written after the publication of the 1649 volume or of verse left over or rejected by Lovelace himself from the earlier book and salvaged after his death by the editors. All we can say is that Lovelace's poetic career spans the two decades from 1636 to 1657—the age of Carew, Suckling, Crashaw, Vaughan, Marvell, Herrick, Cowley, Cleveland, Waller, and, of course, hovering in the background, Milton: the period of the sunset of Carolingian culture, of rising turmoil and civil war, and of Puritan hegemony.

CHAPTER 2

Lute, Canvas, and Trapped Insects: A Poet's Interests

I The Arts

LOVELACE was a minor poet in an age of giants. Though he produced a few gems, his verse is limited in themes or ideas. The difference between Lovelace and his greater contemporaries is partly accounted for by natural endowments—the others were talented individuals, if not outright geniuses, whereas Lovelace was simply a sensitive, well-trained gentleman with a touch of the poet—and partly by manner of life. The code of the gentleman included proficiency in love, or at least in composing love poetry. Lovelace wrote poetry, much of it concerned with love, because doing so, like graceful fencing and dancing, was good form. If he tossed off an excellent lyric, so much the better, but he was not committed day and night to a quest for literary immortality. This sketch of Lovelace's aspiration is, however, only an inference. We have no statement by him of his intentions. As with many seventeenth-century literary figures, none of his personal writings—diary, letters, family papers—is extant. Careful perusal of the poetry discovers only conventional remarks; even his tastes in the literature of his time are deduced with difficulty.

Of his playwriting attempts at Oxford and in the army, all that has survived are a prologue and an epilogue for the London production of *The Scholars*. In the prologue, self-conscious of his university background, he quickly reassures the audience that it need not fear "highbrow" matter:

> Pray, be not frighted, though the scene and gown's
> The University's, the wit's the Town's;
> The lines each honest Englishman may speak,
> Yet not mistake his mother-tongue for Greek,
> For still 'twas part of his vow'd liturgy:
> *From learned comedies deliver me!*
>
> (275, 3–8)

He is likewise conscious of his novitiate: "Then [he] blushes like a virgin now to be/ Robb'd of his comical virginity/ In presence of you all" (15–17).

In the epilogue he takes note of the two kinds of audience that viewed his play: on the one hand, the gallery, which, like Shakespeare's groundlings, loves gross stage effects "in which the throne,/To their amazement, should descend alone,/The rosin lightning flash" (276, 11–13). On the other hand, the gentlemen of the pit, who respond more to subtleties and refinements "like to themselves all spirit, fancy, wit,/In which plots should be as subtle as a flame" (16–17). The writer's task is the difficult one of gaining the applause equally of the "hardened, sooty, and the snowy hand." The man "whose gain" is all his "pleasure" must please as well the town wits and their condescension toward scholars' plays. But Lovelace, contemptuous of the mere playgoer, "Culls out the few, the worthy, at whose feet/He sacrifices both himself and it/His fancy's first fruits. Profit he knows none" (35–37).

A similar aristocratic scorn appears in conjunction with his reverent reference to Sir Philip Sidney, the man to whom later writers were to compare him. Lovelace contrasts "heav'nly Sidney" with "some odd romance so new" (247, 19, 21); "Celestial Sidney's *Arcady*" with the popular, contemporary, endless romances which use "reams of paper" for "Amadis, Sir Guy and Topaz" (277, 2; 286, 40–41). We see, then, the young man of taste, who scorns the vulgar flocking to see crude stage effects and dosing themselves with the endless love romances, and who turns instead to the refinements of Sidney and Fletcher yet remains strangely silent on greater writers like Spenser and Shakespeare.

In several places, Lovelace conjoins poetry and music. In the seventeenth century, as in ancient Greece, the two existed symbiotically; poetry was written for singer, instrument, auditors. Many of Lovelace's own poems were set to music and so circulated long before they saw print, or were written for a popular tune, "A la Chabot," "A la Bourbon," "Courante Monsieur." Music itself was actively participated in by many persons, was thought to be effective in treating the emotions and health, and, in the cosmological thinking, was part of the harmony of the heavenly bodies. The distinct and joint powers of word and note are celebrated in the charming "Dialogue" between a lute and a voice.

The two, admiring each other, delineate the peculiar powers which enable each one to move heaven and hell:

Lute. Sing, Laura, sing, whilst silent are the spheres,
 And all the eyes of heaven are turn'd to ears.
Voice. Touch thy dead wood, and make each living tree
 Unchain its feet, take arms, and follow thee.

(338, 1–4)

The paradox is that dead wood—the instrument—animates the living tree; the dead wood gives life to the forest it sprang from. This allusion to the supernatural musical powers of Orpheus and Amphion also evokes the basic mystery of music itself, the mystery adumbrated by Benedict's half-scornful remark, "Is it not strange that sheep's guts should hale souls out of men's bodies?" (*Much Ado About Nothing*, II, iii, 62–63).

In the second stanza, the poet punningly fuses "chords" and "heart [cordium] string," so that "tremble" and "shake" refer on one level to the sympathetic vibration of strings, as though the heart literally contained strings, on another level to the emotional response to the music and, last, to the ornaments of seventeenth-century lute playing:

Voice. Touch the divinity of thy chords, and make
 Each heartstring tremble, and each sinew shake.
Lute. Whilst with your voice you rarefy the air,
 None but an host of angels hover here.

(7–10)

In the third stanza, Lovelace describes the traditional powers of music and song to captivate the non-human world—beasts, angels, demons:

Voice. Touch thy soft lute, and in each gentle thread
 The lion and the panther captive lead.
Lute. Sing, and in heav'n enthrone deposed Love,
 Whilst angels dance, and fiends in order move.

(12–15)

By being played, the strings of the lute in effect become the leashes of the wild beasts they tame.[1]

In such poems and especially in his references to the music of the spheres, Lovelace is generally looking back to older modes of thought. But on the third of the major arts, painting, Lovelace has some well-defined, forward-looking ideas. He himself was among the few Englishmen responding to the new art of the Renaissance. His poetry exhibits a connoisseur's awareness of the work of recent masters, as well as of their biographers, Giorgio Vasari and Carel Vermander.

Two poems addressed to Lely define the new outlook. "To my worthy Friend . . ." praises Lely for turning away from antiquated procedures:

> Not as of old, when a rough hand did speak
> A strong aspect, and a fair face a weak;
> When only a black beard cri'd villain, and
> By hieroglyphics we could understand;
> When crystal typifi'd in a white spot,
> And the bright ruby was but one red spot.
>   (270, 21–26)

Lovelace refers to the inheritance of medieval iconology, of a non-realistic technique in which figurative and moral considerations were of greater import than duplication of physical reality. The visual image was often a personification, a rendering visible, of an abstract idea. Truth would be represented as a naked woman not because anything erotic was intended but because the truth is by essence without adornment or dress. This series of symbolic conventions, which he calls "hieroglyphics," Lovelace rejects in favor of the finer touches of representational realism:

> Thou dost the things orientally the same,
> Not only paint'st its colour, but its flame:
> Thou sorrow canst design without a tear,
> And with the man his very hope or fear;
> So that th' amazed world shall henceforth find
> None but my Lely ever drew a mind.
>   (27–32) [2]

In the 1659 volume appeared another panegyric to Lely, "Painture," a broad-ranging commentary on the state of the arts. As

Keats was to observe of the Grecian urn, Lovelace notes the power of painting to eternize the transient, to overcome time:

> When Beauty once thy virtuous paint hath on,
> Age needs not call her to vermilion;
> Her beams ne'er shed or change like th' hair of day,
> . . . .
> Whilst we wipe off the num'rous score of years,
> And do behold our grandsires as our peers;
> With the first father of our house compare
> We do the features of our new-born heir;
> For though each copied a son, they all
> Meet in thy first and true original.
>   (352, 47–49, 53–58)

Painting not only imitates reality but is actually a form of creation:

>   What princess not
>   But comes to you to have herself begot?
>   . . . .
>   So by your art you spring up in two moons
>   What could not else be form'd by fifteen suns;
>   . . . .
>   O sacred painture; that dost fairly draw
>   What but in mists deep inward poets saw;
>   . . . .
>   Thou that in frames eternity doest bind,
>   And art a written and a bodi'd mind;
>   . . . .
>   That contemplation into matter brought,
>   Bodi'd ideas, and could form a thought.
>   (59–60, 65–66, 89–90, 95–96, 7–8)

Like music, painting leads us beyond ourselves and our imperfect world. "Amyntor's Grove" tells of works by

>   Titian, Raphael, Giorgione,
>   Whose art ev'n Nature hath outdone;
>   For if weak Nature only can
>   Intend, not perfect, what is man,

These certainly we must prefer,
Who mended what she wrought and her.
(280, 31–36)

II   *Insects and Small Beasts*

Lovelace's responsiveness to music and painting is equalled by his interest in certain small creatures, and this observation of nature constitutes one of his contributions to seventeenth-century English poetry, although writing about small creatures was not unusual. "Let other poets write of dogs,/Some sing of fleas, or fighting frogs," proclaims James Shirley as he begins a poem on birds. The old belief in the system of correspondences caused the writer to take joy in the small representative thing which mirrored the larger world, the microcosm in which he could study the macrocosm. As Jonson put it, "In small proportions we just beauty see." Lovelace is less concerned with the cosmological import of the creatures he describes, however, than with the curiosity, amusement, and teasing humor which they stimulate. He contemplates their fate with geniality and affection.

These poems fall into two groups: those dealing with a variety of insects (ant, bee, grasshopper, spider, fly), and those with birds and small beasts (falcon, heron, toad, snail). The minute creatures enter some of the amatory poems as part of lavish compliments to the lady, but Lovelace's personal touch really appears in a series of poems describing the creatures for their own sake. In "The Snail," after touching on the moral overtones—"Wise emblem of our politic world,/Sage snail, within thine own self curl'd,/Instruct me softly to make haste,/Whilst these my feet go slowly fast" (321, 1–4)—the poet concentrates with good humor on its strange movements:

Compendious snail! thou seem'st to me
Large Euclid's strict epitome;
And, in each diagram, dost fling
Thee from the point unto the ring.
A figure now triangular,
An oval now, and now a square;
And then a serpentine dost crawl,
Now a straight line, now crook'd, now all.
(5–12)

As Robin Skelton notes, Lovelace nicely brings out the touch of absurdity in the snail's ways: "Thou thine own daughter, then, and sire,/That son and mother art entire" (27–28). With mock solemnity, the poet sings of the snail's thrift and religious virtues, its self-containedness. In another poem on the same subject, Lovelace returns to the ridiculousness of the creature with a mock-heroic invocation:

> The centaur, siren, I forgo,
> Those have been sung, and loudly too;
> Nor of the mixed sphinx I'll write,
> Nor the renown'd hermaphrodite:
> Behold, this huddle doth appear
> Of horses, coach, and charioteer;
> That moveth him by traverse law,
> And doth himself both drive and draw;
> Then, when the sun the south doth win,
> He baits him hot in his own inn.
>   (323, 1–10)

Even more stimulating than the snail was the ant, which elicited from Lovelace one of the best of these poems. "The Ant" begins with an indulgent, teasing address to the hardworking creature:

> Forbear, thou great good husband, little ant;
>   A little respite from thy flood of sweat!
> Thou, thine own horse and cart, under this plant
>   Thy spacious tent, fan thy prodigious heat;
> Down with thy double load of that one grain!
> It is a granary for all thy train.
>   (320, 1–6)

The figurative significance is underlined, "Cease, large example of wise thrift, a while,/(For thy example is become our law)" (7–8); the aim is not to convert us to the ant's austerity but to teach the ant—and ourselves—the value of relaxation:

> And teach thy frowns a seasonable smile:
>   So Cato sometimes the nak'd Florals saw.

· · · · · · · · · · · · · · · ·

> Austere and cynic! not one hour t' allow,
>   To lose with pleasure what thou got'st with pain,
> But drive on sacred festivals thy plough,
>   Tearing highways with thy o'ercharged wain.
> Not all thy lifetime one poor minute live,
> And thy o'erlabour'd bulk with mirth relieve?
>   (9–10, 19–24)

The ant is reminded of its natural enemies waiting to destroy it and the fruit of its hard work:

> Look up, then, miserable ant, and spy
>   Thy fatal foes, for breaking of her law,
> Hov'ring above thee: Madam—Margaret Pie,
>   And her fierce servant, Meagre—Sir John Daw;
> Thyself and storehouse now they do store up,
> And thy whole harvest too within their crop.
>   (24–30)

In the last stanza, the poet enlarges the scope of the discussion by including all human endeavor. He had done the same at the outset of "The Snail"; here, however, having been cozened into enjoying a charming description of quaint nature, we are suddenly confronted with the truth of our mortality, in an unexpected place:

> Thus we unthrifty thrive within earth's tomb
>   For some more rav'nous and ambitious jaw:
> The grain in th' ant's, the ant's in the pie's womb,
>   The pie in th' hawk's, the hawk's in th' eagle's maw:
> So scattering to hoard 'gainst a long day,
> Thinking to save all, we cast all away.
>   (31–36)

This conclusion recalls Aesop's fables and Hamlet's reflections in the graveyard as well as his remarks to Claudius on the king's progress through the guts of a worm, and it looks ahead to Burns's moral in "To a Mouse" and to Tennyson's unease at the tableau of "Nature red in tooth and claw." The vanity of human endeavors; the return of dust to dust; the analogy between the ant's predicament and ours ("as flies to wanton boys are we to the gods"); the bitter war of nature—these great themes are sounded genially and in an unfaltering voice.

The ant's industrious life, touched on by the Proverbs of Solomon and by Horace (Satire I, i), was often juxtaposed, in fable, with the grasshopper's insouciance. Popularized in the Middle Ages, dialogues between the two insects recurred in French literature down to La Fontaine. Lovelace himself presented the somewhat different fate of the happy grasshopper: it is overtaken by the cycle of the seasons. The poem on this subject is even more fraught with moral application, but the discussion of its full philosophic scope belongs in the next chapter. It suffices to note now its similarity in tone to Lovelace's other insect and beast lyrics:

> O thou that swing'st upon the waving hair
>   Of some well-filled oaten beard,
> Drunk ev'ry night with a delicious tear
>   Dropt thee from heav'n, where now th' art rear'd:
>
> The joys of earth and air are thine entire,
>   That with thy feet and wings dost hop and fly;
> And when thy poppy works thou dost retire
>   To thy carv'd acorn-bed to lie.
>
>   (259, 1–8)

The poet's joys are at one with the insect's, but then the horizon becomes overcast:

> But ah the sickle! golden ears are cropt;
>   Ceres and Bacchus bid good night;
> Sharp frosty fingers all your flow'rs have topt,
>   And what scythes spar'd, winds shave off quite.
>
> Poor verdant fool, and now green ice!
>   (13–17)

Despite the grasshopper's cheerful character, its doom is like the ant's; and both reflect the human experience: "Thy joys,/ . . . Bid us lay in 'gainst winter rain" (17, 19).

A more frequently observed disaster overtakes the common housefly—entrapment. Lovelace refers to this state a half-dozen times, as when describing the plight of the unrequited low-born lover, "This heard, sir, play still in her eyes,/ And be a-dying lives, like flies/ Caught by their angle-legs and whom/ The torch laughs piecemeal to consume" (283, 62–65). Another "Song" turns the analogy around and uses it in a negative sense: the mistress does *not* behave like a fly: "Strive not, vain lover, to be fine,/ . . . You lessen to a fly your mistress' thought,/To think it may be in a cobweb caught" (312, 1, 3–4).

An insect is ingeniously worked into another sort of love poem, "A Black Patch on Lucasta's Face." In order to turn a graceful compliment, the poet forwards a fanciful explanation of the presence of this fashionable beauty mark: "Dull as I was, to think that a court fly/Presum'd so near her eye,/When 'twas th' industrious bee/Mistook her glorious face for Paradise" (317, 1–4). The bee settles near her eyes, and soon

> Acts the romantic phoenix' fate:
> . . . .
> Chaf'd he's set on fire,
> And in these holy flames doth glad expire;
> And that black marble tablet there,
> So near her either sphere,
> Was plac'd: nor foil, nor ornament,
> But the sweet little bee's large monument.
> (11, 18–23) [3]

The entrapment of the fly or the death of the bee delineates the plight of the lover. The image is developed at length in a different manner in "A Fly about a Glass of Burnt Claret." This concoction of paradoxes toys with the idea of alcoholic beverage as a potent "fire water." Again the poet addresses the insect in the voice of a friendly, experienced counselor: "Forbear this liquid fire, fly,/It is more fatal than the dry,/That singly, but embracing, wounds,/And this at once both burns and drowns" (336, 1–4). To drive his point home, he amusingly catalogues the wines' effects on all sorts of unlikely people:

> 'Tis this makes Venus' altars shine,
> This kindles frosty Hymen's pine;
> When the Boy grows old in his desires,
> This flambeau doth new light his fires.
> . . . .
> The Vestal drinking this doth burn.
> (17–20, 25)

The fly disregards the kindly warning:

> Dost thou the fatal liquor sup,
> One drop, alas! thy bark blows up.
>
> . . . .
> And now th' art fall'n magnanimous fly,
> In, where thine ocean doth fry,
> Like the Sun's son who blush'd the flood
> To a complexion of blood.
>
> (35–36, 41–44)

The poet compassionately comes to the rescue: "Yet see! my glad auricular [=small finger]/Redeems thee (though dissolv'd) a star;/ . . . /See! in the hospital of my hand/Already cur'd, thou fierce dost stand" (45–46, 51–52). The poem concludes with a surprising turn, for the fly, not learning from its debacle, returns for more: "Burnt insect! dost thou reaspire/The moist-hot glass and liquid fire?/I see! 'tis such a pleasing pain,/Thou wouldst be scorched and drown'd again" (53–56). The fly confronting the large glass of the burning liquid—and love is often described as a fire—is all too human: its shock and relapse are ours.

Lovelace's interest in the helpless insect prompted him to translate two of Martial's epigrams on the subject: VI, xv, on an ant embedded in amber; and IV, xxxii, on a bee in honey (372). The creatures' last moments are marked by desperate struggles. The gnat or bee "who, trapp'd in her [spider's] prepared toil,/To their destruction keep a coil" (344, 187–88). In fact, such a predicament becomes the subject of "A Fly Caught in a Cobweb." Like the poems on the snail and the ant, this poem is moralizing, genial, playful. The human import is brought out in the first lines:

> Small type of great ones, that do hum
> Within this whole world's narrow room,
> That with a busy hollow noise
> Catch at the people's vainer voice,
>
> . . . .
> Poor fly caught in an airy net.
>
> (335, 1–4, 7)

The fly's peculiar disaster depicts nicely enough man's predicament, one wrought by his aspiring nature: "Thy wings have fet-

ter'd now thy feet" (8). The fly had managed well so far to escape
a common doom of insects, the flame, only to be overtaken by
another, the spider. The fly's desperate motions—again detailed
by Lovelace—hardly move the confident, lordly spider:

> Where, like a lion in a toil,
> Howe'er, thou keep'st a noble coil,
> And beat'st thy gen'rous breast, that o'er
> The plains thy fatal buzzes roar,
> Till thy all-belli'd foe, round elf,
> Hath quarter'd thee within himself.
>   (9–14)

The fly suffers a death that is not only ignominious in itself but
also, because of its consequences, hideous and diverting:

> But now devour'd art like to be
> A net spun for thy family,
> And, straight expanded in the air,
> Hang'st for thy issue too a snare.
> Strange witty death, and cruel ill,
> That killing thee, thou thine dost kill!
> . . . .
> Thou art thine en'my's sepulchre,
> And in thee buriest too thine heir.
>   (31–36, 39–40)

The analogy between insect and man breaks down here because
there is nothing in human endeavors that quite corresponds to this
horrible fate; the poet has moved beyond the human significance
of the fly's death to the amusing, ironic aspects of the incident
itself. The poetic naturalist has taken over from the moralist.
Something is nevertheless salvaged from the fly's disaster:

> Yet Fates a glory have reserv'd
> For one so highly hath deserv'd;
> As the rhinoceros doth die
> Under his castle-enemy,
> As through the crane's trunk throat doth speed
> The asp doth on his feeder feed;

> Fall yet triumphant in thy woe,
> Bound with the entrail of thy foe.
>
> (41–48)

The fly's death amid its enemy's entrails (the cobweb) is so close to the epic description of the dying warrior's piercing his opponent's belly and dying in the other's entrails—dying on his foe, "going down swinging"—as to allow the poet to dignify by means of sophistry the fly's fate.

We note here Lovelace's keen sense of the natural enmities in the world order. Not only the fly and the spider but also the rhinoceros and the elephant, the crane and the asp, and, earlier, the ant and the magpie or daw, the magpie and the hawk, the hawk and the eagle—all are figures locked in mortal combat. A lengthy poem is devoted entirely to describing another duel involving a spider, "The Toad and Spider." The poet sides with the insect: "First from his den rolls forth that load/Of spite and hate, the speckl'd toad" (9–10). In the manner of the epic hero, Arachne prays to Athene for help. The request is granted. The battle begins as, dodging the toad's breath, "On the toad's blue-chequer'd skull/The spider gluttons herself full,/And vomiting her Stygian seeds,/Her poison" (61–64). The toad shakes her off, rushes to a curative herb for relief, and "then with repeated strength, and scars/That, smarting, fire him to new wars,/Deals blows" (75–77). Avoiding a shot of the toad's spume, the spider makes some headway: "One eye she hath spit out/. . . /And one eye wittily spar'd, that he/Might but behold his misery" (131, 133–34). The swelling toad again totters to his curative herb; but, through the intercession of Athena and the spider's "lar" or household god, the plant has been removed. "The all-confounded toad doth see/His life fled with his remedy" (167–68). He dies with a "dismal horrid yell," and the spider celebrates a triumph. Thus ends a counterpart, according to Mario Praz, of the nightmarish inventions of contemporary Dutch painters and, in its way, a curio of dark humor.[4]

An equally ferocious battle, this time between a falcon and a heron, is described in "The Falcon." The invocation laments man's earthbound state:

> Fair princess of the spacious air,
> That hast vouchsaf'd acquaintance here,

With us [who] are quarter'd below stairs,
That can reach heav'n with naught but pray'rs;
Who, when our activ'st wings we try,
Advance a foot into the sky.

(325, 1–6)

The battle is initiated as, exiled by dogs, "The heron mounted
doth appear/On his own Peg'sus a lancier" (43–44). Each pre-
pares himself with his peculiar tactics:

And now he takes the open air,
Draws up his wings with tactic care,
Whilst th' expert falcon swift doth climb
In subtle mazes serpentine.

(49–52)

The falcon takes the offensive; the heron, "resolv'd to fall/His and
his en'my's funeral" (73–74), counterattacks lethally but is in turn
mortally wounded: "Whilst her [falcon's] own bells in the sad
fall/Ring out the double funeral" (89–90). Siding with the aristocratic bird, Lovelace describes its funeral as attended by the vari-
eties of hawk and proclaims its immortality.[5]

To see the duel poems in perspective, we must recall, to begin
with, the example of the pseudo-Homeric *Battle of the Frogs and
Mice;* for Lovelace clearly uses mock-heroic devices. In such writing, the deadly combat depicted in epics like the *Iliad* is brought
to a level less fraught with import and consequence. With warring
animals and insects rather than human heroes, levity and parody
become apposite. Lovelace is not likely, however, to have been
much influenced by the ancient Greek parody.

The writing of these poems is to be attributed rather to an interest in conflict. Wherever exists amplitude of life, in meadow,
forest, jungle, there obtains destructive competition, struggle,
suffering. Man is deeply, perhaps morbidly, fascinated by such
struggle; and Lovelace in effect presents in his animal poetry a
detached, esthetic picture of conflict, viewed amorally, as a basic
law of brutal Nature. Perhaps for that reason he confines himself
to beasts; in human affairs, the gratuitous, universal lust for combat is usually masked with alleged issues, principles, ideals.

These duel poems also grow out of Lovelace's general interest in animal nature. Though no "nature" poet, he expressed a sympathy for animals that was rare in those days. Geoffrey Walton speaks of Lovelace as being, in these poems, "Something of a naturalist as well as a chivalrous Kentish squire" who blends his gentleman's private interest in animals, field sports, and heraldry with poetic tradition and expresses the rural roots of the Cavalier.[6] There exists, in fact, a tradition of poetry about small animals: Aesop's fables, Virgil's "Gnat," poems in the *Greek Anthology*, the medieval Renard tales, Chaucer's "Nun's Priest's Tale" and "Parliament of Fowls," and, later, the fables of La Fontaine ("The Grasshopper and the Ant"). In such works, however, the emphasis is often satiric or allegorical; the human characteristics the animals represent usually predominate over their lifelike animal traits. Lovelace remains, on the other hand, close to observed facts, so that sometimes, as in the "Snail" or "Fly Caught," the creature's plight is examined even when it ceases to parallel human affairs.

Although, as Kitty Scoulay suggests, Lovelace sometimes lapses into exaggeration, didacticism and bombast, he masters the challenge of limited form presented by such a subject matter. For Robin Skelton, Lovelace approximates Suckling and Carew by using a mock-heroic tone which implies amusement at the solemnities of conventional verse, awareness of the discrepancy between fine words and their artificiality, and duplicity in moralizing while at the same time poking fun at his audience's earnestness. Hugh Kenner best states Lovelace's contribution: "Men would be the poorer had they nothing to say about the doom of flies, and Lovelace's real subject is the human glory of his own loquacious wit, neither teaching nor moving but simply, on each amenable occasion, distinguishing by speech men from the brutes." [7]

At the same time, we must not overemphasize the cheerfulness of tone. The small creatures are constantly dueling, overtaken by adversity, trapped. The image of the trapped insect is related to Lovelace's obsession with prison and confinement. Bruce King, who has stressed with some justice the *angst*-ridden side of Lovelace, finds these poems distrustful, violent, and paranoiac in their reaction to society. Lovelace presents a natural world filled with images of distasteful reality: the fly is emblematic of prominent personages; the snail, of the politic world; the ant, of puritanical austerity now become "our Law." The law of animal life in this insecure world is the law of man: "Us small ants" (356, 62).[8]

Lovelace is clearly no innovator in this manner of writing; he merely handles it better than virtually anyone else. The possible influences on him are varied: the Dutch still-life paintings he saw during his travel years; the late Renaissance emblem books by such as Alciati and Camerarius, and the Latin anthologies by Gruter and Dornavius; the animal verses of the Pléiades poets (Joachim Du Bellay, Remy Belleau, and, notably, Pierre de Ronsard); the epitaphs, elegies, descriptions, narratives, and emblems written by various poets in what a student of the subject has called "the golden age of animal poetry in England"; and, always before these works, the *Greek Anthology* lyrics on locust and cicada, on the strange death of animals, on the contest of raven and scorpion, poems whose tone Lovelace caught and improved.

Nothing in the seventeenth century—not quite Drayton's or Herrick's "fairy-land" poems, certainly not Donne's ratiocinative seduction poem, "The Flea"—is similar. In the eighteenth century, not Blake's cryptic "The Fly" but Burns's seriocomic addresses to a louse and a mouse and Cowper's animal poems are analogous. Not until the poems of Marianne Moore and especially Robert Frost do we come upon a like tone of voice—the humorous, whimsical, observant, teasing, casual tone of Frost's "Fireflies in the Garden," "The White-Tailed Hornet," "To a Moth Seen in Winter," "Departmental," "The Considerable Speck." Frost too treats the little creatures gently, with amusement and solicitous advice; he too notes their unhappy fate, with an "under the aspect of eternity" view that implicitly brings man into the equation. That is the burden of, say, the rather frightening Frost sonnet, "Design," about the result of duel of moth and spider. The two poets are clearly kindred spirits, though Frost possesses a sense of humor, an ingenuity, a rhetoric, above all a sense of relevance, a perceptiveness, a realism about both animal behavior and human feelings that Lovelace could but reach for.

CHAPTER 3

"The Music of Your Chains":
A Poet's Philosophy

I *Christian and Stoic*

ALTHOUGH a staunch defender of king and established church, Lovelace wrote no devotional poems and little that touches on Christianity. In this respect he is nearly alone in an age when even such secular-minded men as Jonson, Herrick, Carew, and Marvell composed in verse an occasional prayer or confessional. If we may judge from his poetry, Lovelace was the sort of Royalist who regards religion as an institution of practical importance for the maintenance of the fabric of society but allows it as little as possible to impinge on his own way of life.

In the occasional poems written for the death of acquaintance or friend, some Christian consolation appears, of course, as it would in the works of all but defiant atheists. Yet these references, as in the elegy on the Princess Katherine, lack depth of conviction or insight; Lovelace introduces the religious imagery in order to continue the tissue of paradoxes that is the core of the poem. The elegy on the death of Cassandra Cotton is the only other poem with any Christian overtones: "Remove this earth/To its last death and first victorious birth" (290, 7–8). The fifty-year-old lady who died a virgin is presented as a saintly example to all young virgins:

> Dare but live like her:
> Dare to live virgins.
> . . . .
> Whilst not a blemish or least stain is seen
> On your white robe 'twixt fifty and fifteen;
> But as it in your swathing-bands was given,
> Bring 't in your winding-sheet unsoil'd to heav'n.
> (27–28, 30–33)

In effective lines, the poet paints a picture of the Christian life as
lived, say, at Little Gidding and as celebrated by George Herbert:

> Dare to affect a serious holy sorrow,
> To which delights of palaces are narrow,
> And lasting as their smiles, dig you a room
> Where practise the probation of your tomb,
> With ever-bended knees and piercing pray'r
> Smooth the rough pass through craggy earth to air.
>   (38–43)

He concludes with the basic Christian paradox of life: "You are
more dead and buried than she" (60).

When one of Lovelace's brothers was killed in action, the poet
addressed lines of consolation to another brother, Francis, "Im-
moderately Mourning My Brother's Untimely Death." In these,
dealing with so personal a grief, eschewing paradox or compliment, Lovelace makes use of no Christian consolation whatever.
The poem is instead wholly Stoic in outlook. Indeed, secular philosophy seems to have meant more to Lovelace than Christianity
as a way of meeting the difficulties of life, for his casual Christian
references pale before the greater intensity found in numerous
poems with a marked Stoic or Epicurean outlook. That Stoicism
interested Lovelace is indicated as well by his translating from
Seneca's Latin some lines of the Greek Stoic, Cleanthes.

The poem to Francis attempts to assuage with Stoic control
their grief over brother William's death. It is a paraphrase of a
Latin elegy by Sarbiewski which was imitated and translated by
many others in the seventeenth and eighteenth centuries. Lovelace's version is curt, well turned. Its burden is that weeping
merely swells grief and that the wise man should accede to fate's
decrees:

> If tears could wash the ill away,
> A pearl for each wet bead I'd pay;
> But as dew'd corn the fuller grows,
> So water'd eyes but swell our woes.
>
> . . . .
>
> Iron decrees of Destiny
> Are ne'er wip'd out with a wet eye.

> But this way you may gain the field,
> Oppose but sorrow, and 'twill yield;
> One gallant thorough-made resolve
> Doth starry influence dissolve.
>
> (289, 1–4, 15–20)

The references to Fate, the Iron decrees of Destiny, the starry influence; the emphasis on resolve, firmness, opposition to grief—all these are an elaboration of the line from Cleanthes, "Fates lead the willing, but unwilling draw" (369, 5).[1]

A different sort of adversity confronts the persona of "A Forsaken Lady." She addresses a young man whom she loves but who has been pursuing another lady to no avail. Though weeping over him, she enjoys seeing him trapped in the same unrequited love that tortures her. But then she changes her tone—her emotions are freezing up; she hardens, masters herself: "But I am chang'd! Bright reason/ . . ./ Hath reach'd me pow'r to scorn as well as thee:/Hail, holy cold! chaste temper, hail!" (257, 31, 34–35). She has achieved the Stoic apathy, which is here fused with the image of the Petrarchan cold, haughty lady.

The Stoic posture is evoked in Lovelace's description of a portrait by Lely of Charles I and his son, who were painted at Hampton Court in the midst of the rising political turmoil and who therefore had much to be resigned to:

> See! what a clouded majesty, and eyes
> Whose glory through their mist doth brighter rise!
> See! what an humble bravery doth shine,
> And grief triumphant breaking through each line!
> How it commands the face! so sweet a scorn
> Never did happy misery adorn!
>
> (269, 1–6)

It might be said that king and son are trying to cheer each other, or that Lely—and Lovelace in turn—is trying to cheer them all, everyone working hard at the proverbial "stiff upper lip," at pose instead of poise.

II *Epicurean*

It is sometimes difficult to separate the moral judgments of the two schools of ancient philosophy, Epicureanism and Stoicism, when dealing with lyric poetry. The ideal of detachment symbolized by Epicurus's modest and austere life outside Athens seems not so distant, at first glance, from the Stoic's self-control, for both Stoics and Epicureans are wary of the passions. Nor is, as Maren-Sofie Røstvig points out in *The Happy Man*, retirement exclusively an Epicurean goal. While valuing man's obligations to society, Stoicism also emphasizes occasional retirement for self-dependence and dignified work, especially when society's adversities become insuperable. The Stoic is, however, deeply conscious of his honor and dignity. He strives for a condition of *apatheia*, of suppression of emotions and personal aspirations, in order to discharge his social responsibilities and to persevere with a decorous austerity under duress, whereas the Epicurean seeks an *ataraxia*, or disengagement from society and all responsibilities. The key difference, then, is that Stoicism aims for a balance between the active and contemplative lives and that Epicureanism seeks only the second.[2]

Lovelace is a poet, not a philosopher; and his "philosophic" positions are instinctual responses, not reasoned choices. A Lovelace poem may be Stoic or Epicurean in the sense that a man who never read a book of philosophy may be Stoic if he says, "I must finish the work before I take the vacation," or an Epicurean if he says, "To hell with the work: I'm going on vacation now!" If we judge by the number of poems, Lovelace was attracted more to the Epicurean position, to the drink imbibed with a flourish of insouciance; but he also had his Stoic moments. Most writers, in any case, are not all one or the other but have moods in which either attitude dominates.

Thus, when about to present himself to the hardened London theater audience as a playwright for the first time, Lovelace stoically steels himself for probable rejection. Satisfied with what he has written and content to have it understood by "the few, the worthy," he seeks no other gain or pleasure: "Profit he knows none,/Unless that of your approbation" (277, 37–38). On the other hand, when someone else's aspirations come into play, it is easier to strike a contented Epicurean note. Thus the hardworking, dutiful ant is urged to turn from duty to pleasure; or the poet's brother Francis is exhorted, on the occasion of a trip abroad, to think of comfort in lieu of ambition:

> Frank, wilt live handsomely? trust not too far
> Thyself to waving seas;
> . . . .
> Yet settle here your rest, and take your state,
> . . . .
>   Nay, steadfast stand,
> As if discover'd were a New-found-land.
>   (348, 1–2, 5, 9–10)

The sea is treacherous and dangerous; even the seemingly settled earth, we now know, moves wildly; and its movement is symbolic of the giddy whirl of human life and society. The solution is not for man to place himself at the mercies of the even more uncertain seas but to look within, to contract his desires and needs, to settle for the moderate:

> To rear an edifice by art so high
> That envy should not reach it with her eye,
> Nay, with a thought come near it—wouldst thou know
> How such a structure should be rais'd? build low.
>   (37–40)

With proper resolution, he can withstand all: "A breast of proof defies all shocks of fate" (47).

The idea of the golden mean here expressed is central to Horace's fusion of Aristotelian ethics with Epicurean retirement and mild pleasure-seeking. The poem is indeed deeply influenced by Horace; and Katherine McEuen, a student of Classical influences on English poetry, finds it an excellent paraphrase typical of the vein of Classicism in Lovelace's work. He follows the Latin closely, except when interpolating a thought (like the reference to the earth's movement) which applies Horace to the modern situation.[3]

Unabashed Epicurean, even hedonistic, expressions abound in Lovelace's work, notably in the dozen or so poems celebrating drink. Man has always responded ambivalently to alcoholic beverages; at once boon and bane, they liberate him while also unmanning him in several ways. The ambivalence is reflected in the way most people boast of their intoxication, whether rare or frequent, and in the large number of slang and colloquial expres-

sions for drunkenness. Hence a half-smirking allusive tone properly characterizes the poem "The Fly About a Glass of Burnt
Claret." The fiery quality of the liquid is attributable not only to
its being *burnt* claret but also to its taste and effects. The fly's
debacle in falling into it is our debacle: "I see! 'tis such a pleasing
pain,/Thou wouldst be scorch'd and drown'd again" (337, 55–56).
The paradoxes in the poem—"liquid fire," "scorch'd and drown'd,"
"pleasing pain"—are so many jokes on inebriation and ambivalence.

The positive, restorative qualities of wine are celebrated in the
bacchanalian "A Loose Saraband [1659]." A saraband was a slow
Spanish dance then popular, and the title indicates the tune to
which the words were written. Though the text of a similarly
titled poem in the 1649 volume has nothing to do with dancing,
this lyric of 1659 may have been written specifically for a dancing
occasion: "Nay, prithee dear, draw nigher,/Yet closer, nigher yet"
(324, 1–2). Influenced ultimately by Anacreon's joint praises of
wine and love, the poem renders somewhat more unto Bacchus
than unto Venus:

> Here is a double fire,
>   A dry one and a wet.
> True lasting heavenly fuel
> Puts out the vestal jewel,
> When once we twining marry
> Mad love with wild canary.
>   (3–8)

The drunk, like the lover, projects onto the world his feelings:

> See all the world, how 't staggers,
>   More ugly drunk than we,
> As if far gone in daggers
>   And blood it seem'd to be:
> We drink our glass of roses,
> Which naught but sweets discloses,
> Then, in our loyal chamber,
> Refresh us with love's amber.
> . . . .
> What of Elysium's missing?
> Still drinking and still kissing.
>   (25–32, 37–38)

The paean comes to a memorable climax with the question, "Lord! what is man and sober?" (40). The two entities "man" and "sobriety" are mutually exclusive. Lovelace takes the usual definition of man as a rational creature and mischievously suggests that the reverse is true, that only drunken reasonlessness brings out true manliness.

The poem is rounded off with a carefree, glowing conclusion:

> Now is there such a trifle
>   As honour, the fool's giant?
> What is there left to rifle,
>   When wine makes all parts pliant?
> Let others glory follow,
> In their false riches wallow,
> And with their grief be merry:
> Leave me but love and sherry.
>   (41–48)

The ridicule of honor and glory is reminiscent of similar sallies by Falstaff or by the persona of Donne's lyrics and anticipates such poems as Burns's "Jolly Beggars." Such ridicule, together with the hedonistic abandonment to wine and to the love that follows, expresses a side of Lovelace less known than his Cavalier steadfastness in "To Althea" and his devotion to honor in "To . . . Wars."

Drink is equally important in the soldier's life. The capacity to ingest it deeply is, in such a milieu, as much a touchstone of masculinity as swordplay or sexual prowess. Hence it is natural to find Lovelace writing, at the time of the disastrous Pacification of Berwick, a poetic toast to his chief, General Goring. Despite—or perhaps because of—the fact that the peace is made on the enemy's terms, Lovelace turns for solace from war to drink, with the somewhat Isaiah-like image of helmets changing into kettles.

Drink is also a stimulant of friendly intercourse and witticisms, a cement of friendship. It is therefore prominent in a visit to the country house of an old friend; after arrival and sightseeing, Lovelace relaxes with his host: "We bound our loose hair with the vine,/The poppy and the eglantine;/One swell'd an oriental bowl/ . . . /So drench'd we our oppressing cares" (280, 55–57, 67). A similar quiet communion with a friend takes place under less auspicious circumstances in "The Grasshopper." Lovelace addresses Charles Cotton as the winter of political discontent and turmoil settles over the land—gone are the bluster, camaraderie and gregarious abandonment of the military toast, the loosening of inhibitions in an erotic situation, or the effusive joys of a country visit. The grasshopper's happy but transient existence bears a lesson for the two friends:

> Poor verdant fool, and now green ice! thy joys,   •
>   Large and as lasting as thy perch of grass,
> Bid us lay in 'gainst winter rain, and poise
>   Their floods with an o'erflowing glass.
>   (259, 17–20)

Wine is a balance against the floods of rain; friendship and continent private pleasure, against public disaster. Like the grasshopper, which was "drunk ev'ry night with a delicious tear,"

> Thou best of men and friends! we will create
> A genuine Summer in each other's breast.
>
> . . . .
> Dropping December shall come weeping in,
>   Bewail th' usurping of his reign;
> But when in show'rs of old Greek we begin,
>   Shall cry he hath his crown again.
>   (21–22, 29–32)

In this bleak time the poet chooses neither Stoic repression of desires nor adherence to duty in the face of difficulties but withdrawal, endurance through friendship, drink, modest pleasures:

> Night as clear Hesper shall our tapers whip
>   From the light casements where we play,
> And the dark hag from her black mantle strip,
>   And stick there everlasting day.
>   (33–36)

The grasshopper sets for the Cavaliers, which it symbolizes, an example of conviviality. This image has a venerable history, going all the way back to Homer, Hesiod, Plato, Philostratus, Meleager. Among the Greeks, the grasshopper was associated with musicianship and poetry, with noblemen and insouciance, with men in political disfavor—all of which recalls the character and plight of

Lovelace and the Cavaliers. In Renaissance emblem books, the grasshopper symbolized content, hope, fragility. The poem, in effect, sounds the mid-seventeenth-century Royalist retreat from affairs of state, society, and war.

The first three stanzas are an "imitation" of Anacreon and, as such, form an interesting contrast with Abraham Cowley's contemporary version, an Epicurean pastoral with simple diction. Lovelace's poem presents detailed description, subtle rhythms, a gentle tone, and a nice blending of Classical allusions with a colloquial style and an occasional conceit. Where Cowley dwells only on the blissful aspects, Lovelace takes cognizance of the winter of life. Stanzas IV and V lead us to defeat and death, to prudent morality. Then we shift from past to present, from the symbolic history of the grasshopper to immediate history of poet and friend; from Anacreon's vinous exuberance to Horatian ode of direct address on retirement, friendship, nature; to a Cavalier drinking song, with, D. C. Allen suggests in "Lovelace: 'The Grasshopper,'" a tinge of Christianity, of Christian Epicureanism. In privacy and withdrawal, the poet and his friend can create an inward summer that is more real than the winters of Nature and Fate; they can remake the grasshopper's lost summer.

The grasshopper functions in this poem, as a creature free of human anguish and at the same time as a teacher: it knows how to enjoy life even while it makes men merry. And that its brief, colorful life is snuffed out, turned into "green ice," reminds the poet and his friend that the same will happen to them ("We were in our own sight as grasshoppers" [Numbers xiii.33]). As long as they are still alive, however, thoughts of death will spur them into even greater enjoyment of life. They are determined to overcome the external discomfitures by falling back on their own resources and qualities of character, on man's capacity to master fate. The grasshopper is both a warning and a pattern. Insect and man drink, depend on "showers," live best in the light; but the paradox which holds the two halves of the poem together is that men, partaking of the same sort of activity as the insects, are yet lords of their selves and can "poise floods" while the grasshopper is a weak "poor verdant fool."

> Thus richer than untempted kings are we,
> That asking nothing, nothing need:

> Though lord of all what seas embrace, yet he
> That wants himself is poor indeed.
>   (37–40) [4]

The best of both insect and drink poems, "The Grasshopper" is, as critics of the past half century have come to see, very good indeed; it is almost on a par with such related poems as Burns's "To a Mouse," Keats's nightingale ode, and Shelley's "Skylark." Presenting the contemplative side of Lovelace the soldier and lover, it is an evocation of the Cavalier spirit in duress, of the quiet hermitage of the mind, of the eternal summer within in the absence of king and social order without.

III   Prison

This turn to Epicureanism rather than Stoicism in the face of public disaster is also characteristic of poems dealing with a personal disaster, physical confinement. We readily associate Lovelace with jail because he was twice imprisoned and because his single most famous poem deals with the subject. As a matter of fact, images of incarceration, like those of trapped insects, haunted his imagination and appear in even innocent-looking poems. The extreme is no doubt the "witty" torture used in Spanish prisons, one involving confinement within confinement (in "The Toad and Spider"):

> Heretics' bare heads are arm'd
> In a close helm, and in it charm'd
> An overgrown and meagre rat,
> That piecemeal nibbles himself fat.
>   (341, 57–60)

More is revealed of prison life by a simile in "Aramantha,"

> Now, as a prisoner new cast,
> Who sleeps in chains that night his last,
> Next morn is wak'd with a reprieve,
> And from his trance not dream bid live,
> Wonders (his sense not having scope)
> Who speaks, his friend or his false hope.
>   (307, 197–202)

Such a happy experience Lovelace probably knew firsthand; in "The Triumphs," he inserted six clearly autobiographical lines:

> What fate was mine, when in mine obscure cave
> (Shut up almost close prisoner in a grave)
> Your beams could reach me through this vault of night,
> And canton the dark dungeon with light!
> Whence me, as gen'rous spahis, you unbound,
> Whilst I now know myself both free and crown'd.
>
> (344, 7–12)

The exact interpretation of these lines is uncertain;[5] whatever the aid given him, Lovelace must have awakened one day to better conditions in jail and not been able to believe his luck.

But confinement may be spiritual instead of, or as well as, physical: "A Guiltless Lady Imprison'd" contains a series of complimentary paradoxes addressed to a pretty whore:

> See! that which chains you you chain here;
> The prison is thy prisoner;
> How much thy jailor's keeper art!
> He binds your hands, but you his heart.
>
> (288, 5–8)

The lover is bound (323, 3), or possessed ("The Scrutiny," "Wars"); he is akin to a misguided bee or trapped fly. Night to him is the

> Loathed jailor of the lock'd-up sun,
> And tyrant-turnkey on committed day,
> Bright eyes lie fetter'd in thy dungeon,
> And heaven itself doth thy dark wards obey,
>
> (314, 1–4)

and equally constricting is another fact of daily life, clothing:

> **Love's martyrs of the town,**
> **All day imprison'd in a gown,**
> **Who, rack'd in silk 'stead of a dress,**
> **Are clothed in a frame or press,**

> And with that liberty and room
> The dead expatiate in a tomb.
>   (303, 15–20)

Amarantha is urged to let her hair fly "unconfin'd," even as in the golden age the young lovers were "unconfined." But now "Will I fling all at her feet I have,/My life, my love, my very soul a slave?/Tie my free spirit only unto her,/And yield up my affection prisoner?" (275, 89–92). Hence the persona of "To Lucasta. From Prison" is shackled in two ways, to Lucasta as well as to the jail walls. Thrown back upon his resources, he must reconsider his values in a dissolving world. After all the other political institutions fail to pass muster, he consecrates himself anew to the king.

This sober scrutiny of self and body politic is quite different from the two remaining poems on prison life: "The Vintage to the Dungeon" and "To Althea. From Prison." In them, Stoic sentiments are complemented, if not displaced, by Epicurean ones, as the theme of drinking fuses with the theme of prison to produce two of Lovelace's most characteristic and well-known creations. The "Vintage to the Dungeon" is brief and simple:

> Sing out, pent souls, sing cheerfully!
> Care shackles you in liberty,
> Mirth frees you in captivity:
>   Would you double fetters add?
>   Else why so sad?
>
> Chorus: Besides your pinion'd arms you'll find
>   Grief too can manacle the mind.
>
> Live then pris'ners uncontroll'd;
> Drink o' th' strong, the rich, the old,
> Till wine too hath your wits in hold;
>   Then if still your jollity
>   And throats are free—
>
> Chorus: Triumph in your bonds and pains,
>   And dance to th' music of your chains.
>   (263)

This lyric is a rousing assertion of the human capacity to overcome adversity. The paradox of triumphing within man's bonds and pains is rendered vividly concrete in the image of dancing to the chains' music—man turning to good use the very thing that curtails his happiness, making his music where he finds it, letting himself go in the worst of circumstances. The sounds of the chain are transformed by the imagination from a reminder of sorrow into an accompaniment of joy; the very thing which confines man's body liberates his soul. By dancing grief away, the prisoner also effaces the chains; they are not chains if not regarded as such. The impediments are transcended. Thus this simple, lovely couplet best celebrates the power of the imagination.

If, as Willa Evans conjectured in "Lovelace's Concept of Prison Life," "The Vintage to the Dungeon" did not grow out of the poet's prison experiences, the same may hold true of "To Althea. From Prison," which the unreliable Wood associated with Lovelace's 1642 incarceration in Gatehouse.[6]

When Love with unconfined wings
    Hovers within my gates,
And my divine Althea brings
    To whisper at the grates;
When I lie tangled in her hair,
    And fetter'd to her eye,
The gods, that wanton in the air,
    Know no such liberty.

When flowing cups run swiftly round
    With no allaying Thames,
Our careless heads with roses bound,
    Our hearts with loyal flames;
When thirsty grief in wine we steep,
    When healths and draughts go free,
Fishes, that tipple in the deep,
    Know no such liberty.

When, like committed linnets, I
    With shriller throat shall sing
The sweetness, mercy, majesty,
    And glories of my king;
When I shall voice aloud how good
    He is, how great should be;
Enlarged winds, that curl the flood,
    Know no such liberty.

> Stone walls do not a prison make,
>   Nor iron bars a cage;
> Minds innocent and quiet take
>   That for an hermitage;
> If I have freedom in my love,
>   And in my soul am free,
> Angels alone, that soar above,
>   Enjoy such liberty.
>
> (284–85)

The greatest of prison poems, "To Althea. From Prison" defies analysis. As with all great art, its essence is simplicity, seeming artlessness obtained from polish and care. Built on a Cavalier antithesis of bodily confinement and spiritual liberty, it comes to express "the triumph of mind over matter" in words "simple and profound, limpid and musical." The first three stanzas examine the theme in three different ways, each one concluding with the paradox that the imprisoned man has greater liberty than have the free creatures and forces of nature. "Know no such liberty" is the refrain. The three prison pastimes, the means to spiritual freedom and happiness, are the standard ones—women, wine, song—celebrated by hedonists from Anacreon through Goliard and Burns to the latest "Beat" poet; and we recall Franz Hals's "Laughing Cavalier" painting as a perfect analogue to this lyric.

The stanzas are carefully constructed. Each consists of two quatrains, the "b" rhyme (*ee*) of the second quatrain remaining the same throughout the poem. Each of the first three stanzas begins with "when"; the seventh line of each compares the prisoner's state with another creature—gods,[7] fishes, winds, and angels. The joys of the first three fall short of his joys; only angels can match his freedom, for he has become angel-like, a free spirit.

In the first stanza, ideas of freedom and confinement are manipulated paradoxically. The poet lies in jail *"tangled* in her hair" and *"fettered* to her eye" yet thereby is made free by love's "unconfined" wings. The stanza describing, in the manner of "Vintage to the Dungeon," the abandonment to drink is tied to the first and third by its references to the heart "bound" with "loyal flames"— loyal to his mistress Althea and to his king (stanza three), whose praise he will sing. The basic Cavalier themes of love and honor are thus counterpointed with hedonistic delights and with the elusive, protean idea of freedom: man may be "free to" even while not being "free from." The climactic stanza draws the conclusion with memorable generalization, powerful aphoristic lines which round out this brief depiction of the elements of true freedom— constancy to mistress, loyalty to political party, the coziness of good company and potation in jail.[8]

The idea that the mind, not external circumstances, determines man's happiness has found expression in all places and ages. It is the core of Buddha's teaching, of Stoicism, as well as of Christianity ("the Kingdom of Heaven is within you"); it is the ground theme of Horace's Ode I, xxii, and of Boethius' *Consolations of Philosophy;* and it was acted out by the religious martyrs. In English literature alone, the idea was given poetic expression in, for example, Chaucer's "Knight's Tale":

> For elles hadde I dwelled with Theseus,
> Yfetered in his prisoun everemo.
> Thanne hadde I been in blisse, and nat in wo.
> Oonly the sighte of hire whom that I serve,
> Though that I never hir grace may deserve,
> Walde han suffised right ynough for me; . . .

in Shakespeare's *Hamlet:* "I could be bounded in a nutshell and count myself a king of infinite space, were it not that I have bad dreams"; in his *Tempest:*

> My father's loss, the weakness which I feel,
> The wrack of all my friends, nor this man's threats
> To whom I am subdu'd, are but light to me,
> Might I but through my prison once a day
> Behold this maid; . . .

in *As You Like It:* "thought is free"; in Milton's *Paradise Lost,*

> A mind not to be changed by place or time.
> The mind is its own place, and in itself
> Can make a Heaven of Hell, a Hell of Heaven.

> But shalt possess
> A Paradise within thee, happier far; . . .

in Adam's lyric to Eve on the miseries of life without her, and
Samson's rebuke to Dalilah: "The gaol I count the house of Lib-
erty/To [=compared with] thine"; in Wordsworth:

> Nuns fret not at their convent's narrow room;
> And hermits are contented with their cells.
> In truth the prison, into which we doom
> Ourselves, no prison is; . . .

and in Byron, "Eternal Spirit of the chainless Mind!/Brightest in
dungeons, Liberty! thou art." Blake's telling phrase, "mind-forged
manacles," is related to this idea—stone walls do not make a
prison, but the mental shackles (cf. "Grief too can manacle the
mind" [263, 7]) may. So are Thoreau's thoughts while in prison: "I
could not help being struck with the foolishness of that institution
which treated me as if I were mere flesh and blood and bones, to
be locked up. . . . I did not for a moment feel confined, and the
walls seemed a great waste of stone and mortar." Lovelace's poem
was often copied or parodied in the seventeenth century; the idea,
in short, has often been thought but never so well expressed.[9]

   The idea is, in fact, a major theme of Lovelace's poetry. In "Another [on the snail]," he gives a twist to Horace's remark that
wherever man flees to, the heavens are the same:

> But, banished, I admire his fate,
> Since neither ostracism of state,
> Nor a perpetual exile
> Can force this virtue change his soil:
> For wheresoever he doth go,
> He wanders with his country too.
>   (323, 21–26; cf. 260, 39–40)

These lines contain a personal reference; for the defeated,
hounded Royalist envies the snail and its self-sufficiency, its repose, its capacity to remain true to itself; its "prison" is its home.
In "A Guiltless Lady Imprisoned," the beautiful charmer is less
confined than she seems since she actually imprisons her jailor's
heart. The first lines of "To Lucasta. From Prison" request, as we
have seen, freedom from the lady, not from the prison walls. To
"dance to the music of your chains" is to deny confidently the
ultimate reality of prison; for "Care shackles you in liberty,/Mirth

frees you in captivity" (263, 2–3). The poet builds his own world with his values even as the friends in "The Grasshopper" created "everlasting day" and inner summer amid the pervasive night and winter.

The great adversity, throughout Lovelace's work, is entrapment, whether in prison amid political defeat or to a lady. And the problem is whether to deal with it by physical flight; or by ascent to something higher through self-discipline; or by dying like the trapped insect. In "To Althea," the testing by imprisonment of his loyalty and endurance elicits these proud assertions of his devotion to the king. Prison is the acid test of values, loyalty, integrity; it is, to use current expressions, "the moment of truth," the occasion for revealing "grace under pressure." Nor is this a pious wish only. We think of the men, good or evil—Socrates, Raleigh, Bunyan, Hitler, Gandhi, to name but a few—who found themselves and their vocations in prison; who wrote important works there; and who, in their very moments of defeat, confinement, and abasement, triumphed.

Though a Royalist broadside, "To Althea" is ennobled with an air of masculine spontaneity, with a rare note of idealism any reader can respond to. Speaking with the stance, the gestures, peculiar to the poet's time and place—the Cavalier's buoyant flourish of loyalty in the gloom of 1640–60—the poem transcends its historical setting and achieves immortality by capturing the essence of its age, by extracting the universal from the temporal, by making the values of a bygone civilization at its finest come alive.

Though "To Althea" expresses something of the Stoic creed that "Fates lead the willing, but unwilling draw," the sanguine turning from adversity and confinement to joy and inner freedom is helped by wine and the image of the beloved—a situation that smacks not a little of Epicurean values. As Hartmann states in *The Cavalier Spirit*, the idea that jail is no jail if conscience is clear is part of the Cavalier's Epicurean philosophy which found pleasure in any experience not without nobility.[10] Is this uncertainty as to proper labels not evidence of how difficult it sometimes is to distinguish between the two philosophies in lyric poetry? In any case, questions of whether "To Althea" is Stoic or Epicurean vanish before this bold celebration of man's proved ability to confront his adversity, ignore his environment, and master his destiny.

CHAPTER 4

"The Hidden Fate of Princes":
A Poet's Socio-Political Views

I Social and Occasional Poetry

THERE is a poetry which addresses itself to the smaller society of the poet's immediate circle of friends, relatives, and acquaintances. Such *vers de société,* eschewing lyric intensity as well as the broadly satirical and the philosophical, consists usually of nicely turned compliments and expressions of gratitude for small favors or actions. It may incidentally extol the life led by friends and hosts as representative of the best of Christian, English, or aristocratic ways. Such poetry makes from the conventions of social life a subject for art. It can be written only by an insider who has the breeding and intimate acquaintance with the standards of decorous conduct—who has control, ease, elegance, delicacy, lack of pedantry. Not springing from some deep inspiration, the "occasional" poems are written, often in a short time, for a specific event in either the poet's personal life or the life of the realm.

In the personal occasional poem written to a friend, prosaic, trivial details become central. A recently pregnant lady asks for an old shirt, in accord with a venerable superstition; a painting of Lucasta is unveiled; the poet's lady love acquires a muff; he neglected to write a letter when in Rotterdam—such incidents generate informal poems, just as other occasions, visits, favors beget complimentary, quasi-amatory verses addressed to equals. Even the "universal" poems are given by their titles a flavoring of the occasional kind: ". . . Going to the Wars," ". . . Going Beyond the Seas." The poems celebrate the minor pleasures and sadnesses of life. Analogous to the contemporary Dutch genre painting, they present ordinary humanity enjoying its day-to-day affairs. The chance inspirations of a quick intelligence, they exist to entertain. With self-mocking wit, colloquial directness, casual parentheses and changes of tone, they express a suspicion of attitudinizing, a take-it-or-leave-it tone instead of high seriousness.

In more elevated style, the public poems record something done by the king, his family and entourage, or by the courtiers. Births and deaths are celebrated and mourned, respectively, according to clear conventions. The goal of this poetry of ceremony is to compliment and to commemorate the public event, not to express the poet's personal attitude. The task requires considerable skill, and such poets were imaginative in their way. Devoted to the king, moreover, they really believed in his Divine Right; hence the cosmic significance of royal births and deaths. Behind all the rhetoric and exaggeration was a fervent aspiration.

Although written in all ages, both the personal and public occasional poetry, especially the latter, were becoming more prominent in the years 1625–50. Of the public occasional poems touching the royal family, Lovelace wrote only a few samples. "Princess Louisa Drawing" is typical of the genre, for what could, to worldly ears, be more insignificant among the actions surrounding the seat of power than the play of an infant, royal though it be? But because it *is* a princess, the poet embarks on the—legitimate, as it then seemed—attempt to dress up the event, to display his ingenuity in being able to find significance in it, and to wring compliments from it. A different mood necessarily pervades the elegy on Princess Katherine, but technically the difference is not great, for the poem is a tissue of paradoxes, a tour de force meant, like the previous verses on a happier moment in the royal household, to exhibit the poet's resourcefulness.

Of the lyrics dealing with friends and acquaintances, a common type was the country-house poem. This kind obtained in an age when poets were either themselves aristocrats or dependent on noble patrons. L. C. Knights has shown how the work of John Donne, in all its variety and receptivity to ideas, grew out of the aristocratic, ecclesiastical, and administrative milieu in which he moved. The social center was the country house of the noble family, which, as in the case of a place like the immense Knole House, was often a community of its own. Here poets were taken on as tutors or entertained as intellectual equals. This social symbiosis came to an end with the social change effected by the Civil War, but during the first half of the seventeenth century, there thrived a genre of poems by Jonson, Carew, Herrick, Marvell, which celebrated the country houses and their way of life, the roots of the king's court in the land, the patrician class, the English rural scene with its "primitive," uncorrupted virtues.[1]

"Amyntor's Grove," Lovelace's contribution to the genre, is addressed to Endymion Porter, who, as friend and patron of Rubens and Van Dyck, helped Charles I form his fine collection of Renaissance paintings. Lovelace, belonging to both the court and the country-house circles, probably came to know Porter at court or while on the 1639–40 expeditions with General Goring, to whom Porter was related. Over the poem is thrown a thin veil of pastoral figurative language. But the pastoral tradition is nearly dead by the time Lovelace comes to use it, and he has none of Milton's ability to pour new life into it. Some fine lines aside, this lyric does not compare favorably with the others of this genre. The praise remains mere hyperbole because it is not swept up in that description which, not without a sense of humor, transcends the particulars to convey an order of life, a vision of community, a rapport with nature. Lovelace fails to endow the house and family with a philosophic or social significance.

A different home and visit are celebrated in "Being Treated/To Ellinda." The lady's identity is unknown; but, in view of the informal, playful language and intimate tone, she must have been a relative or close friend. The poem expresses gratitude for his being well fed:

> For glasses, heads, hands, bellies full
> Of wine and loin right-worshipful;
> Whether all of, or more behind-a:
> Thanks, freest, freshest, fair Ellinda.
>
> . . . .
> But now to close all I must switch hard,
> Servant ever,
>   *Lovelace Richard.*
>   (285, 11–14, 43–44)

His solemn poetic robes off, Lovelace is *en pantoufles.* Not interested in hyperbolic praise of an aristocratic way of life, he writes with Suckling-like nonchalance an amusing series of octosyllabic couplets containing outrageous inversions and rhymes that remind us of Samuel Butler and Ogden Nash.

One type of occasional poem marks the completion of a painting or publication of a book. Of such a nature are "Painture" (on Lely and the new realism in art), the two poems on Fletcher's plays, and the octosyllabics on a translation of *Clitophon*. The lines for *Pallas Armata*, a book on the gentleman's use of sword and rapier, suggest that its reader will gain both learning and prowess through vicarious, armchair swordsmanship. The point is made by paradox:

> Hark, Reader! wilt be learn'd i' th' wars?
> A general in a gown?
>
> . . . .
> Wouldst be a wonder?
>
> . . . .
> A bishop in a garrison,
> And conquer by the book?
>
> Take then this mathematic shield,
> And henceforth by its rules
> Be able to dispute i' th' field,
> And combat in the schools.
> (278, 1–2, 5, 7–12)

"Conquer by the book" can mean both "vicariously" and "fighting according to the rules and advice here set down." The inversion, "Dispute i' th' field/And combat in the schools," stresses the double benefits. The witty byplay between the real struggles and the vicarious, peaceful ones appears again in "To Dr. F. V. on his Book of Chess."

Interesting as well is his poem for the late John Hall's translation of Hierocles' commentary on Pythagoras' "Golden Verses." Although Hall was one of the very few poets in the seventeenth century to take the Parliamentary side in the Civil War, staunchly Royalist Lovelace praises the man and his work, merely intimating in a single couplet the unfortunate difference in their political outlook: "Alas! our faiths made different essays,/Our minds and merits brake two several ways" (359, 9–10).

II   *Politics: Polemic and Satire*

Lovelace is so well known for his few well-turned lyrics on love, honor, and friendship that most readers are not aware of his poems on the passing social and political scene. His best work, to be sure, does not lie in this area; unlike Jonson and Dryden, he was unable to bring the same poetic forcefulness to public issues as to personal relations. Indeed, it is not easy to tell how emotionally Lovelace was involved with the Civil War, the major public event during his lifetime. He praised, we saw, John Hall and received praise from Marvell, both Roundhead poets. The death of Charles I, furthermore, elicited no elegy from him. A curious detachment is suggested by the pastoral "Aramantha." When the swain and the heroine-shepherdess discover each other's identities and are reunited, she relates her experiences to him,

> Her various chance and diff'ring gate:
> How chas'd by Hydraphil, and track'd,
> The num'rous foe to Philanact,
> Who, whilst they for the same things fight,
> As bards' decrees and druids' rite,
> For safeguard of their proper joys
> And shepherd's freedom, each destroys
> The glory of this Sicily.
>
> (310, 326–33)

For C. H. Wilkinson, these lines clearly refer to the Civil War. Hydraphil, meaning "lover of the many-headed beast," stands for Parliament, and Philanact for the Cavaliers. The fight "for the same things, . . . /bards' decrees and druids' rite" is over the interpretation of the Law (sacred and profane)—handed down by poet-prophet and priest—which both sides in the Civil War claim to uphold. The land destroyed by this selfish scramble is England, not Sicily.

If Wilkinson is correct, the last lines show a detachment by Lovelace, a realization that not only "they" but "we" too are intemperate and destructive; and the ensuing lines beautifully convey the poignancy of unbounded idealism and uncompromising stands leading to civil turmoil:

> Since, seeking thus the remedy,
> They fancy (building on false ground)
> The means must them and it confound,
> Yet are resolv'd to stand or fall,
> And win a little or lose all.
>
> (334–38)

Perhaps Lovelace, like Marvell, more a spectator than a partisan, saw through the claims of each side to the ultimate folly and selfishness in any war, especially fratricidal war so destructive of civilization; but he had not the poetic vision or capacity to express this insight in a poem of the stature of Marvell's "Horatian Ode Upon Cromwell's Return From Ireland."

Various passages in Lovelace's non-political verse possibly allude to domestic strife, but he came to grips with the crisis in only two poems of some intensity and effectiveness: "To Lucasta. From Prison" and "Mock Song." "To Lucasta. From Prison" has less to do with jail or love than with the contemporary social and political scene. Though the other prison poems are perhaps not to be hitched to either of the poet's own confinements, this one clearly bears a personal tone, so personal in fact that, as we noted, its opening lines caused much conjecture over his love life. Actually, the enigmatic first stanza merely provides the reason for the rest of the poem and its quest.

Addressing Lucasta, the poet seeks liberty not from the prison he is in but from the emotional imprisonment inside himself. Mary McCarthy recently stated the matter perfectly, in another connection: "To be in the town jail, as Thoreau knew, can relieve any sense of imaginary imprisonment." [2] Lovelace desires a new object for his devotion. In critical times that is no easy thing to find. Having burned his fingers with unrequited love, he will henceforth devote himself to something only after first testing it with great care. The candidates turn out to be political, and the ensuing eight stanzas constitute a survey of the burning issues of the day and of the social disruptions:

> First I would be in love with Peace,
> And her rich swelling breasts' increase;
> But how, alas! how may that be,
> Despising earth, she will love me?
>
> Fain would I be in love with War,
> As my dear just avenging star;
> But War is lov'd so ev'rywhere,
> Ev'n he disdains a lodging here.
>
> Thee and thy wounds I would bemoan,
> Fair thorough-shot Religion;

> But he lives only that kills thee,
> And whoso binds thy hands is free.
>
> I would love a Parliament
> As a main prop from heav'n sent;
> But ah! who's he that would be wedded
> To th' fairest body that's beheaded?
>
> Next would I court my Liberty,
> And then my birthright, Property;
> But can that be, when it is known
> There's nothing you can call your own?
>   (265, 9–28)

"Reformation," a key word, is aptly interpreted here:

> A Reformation I would have,
> As for our griefs a sov'reign salve;
> That is, a cleansing of each wheel
> Of state, that yet some rust doth feel;
>
> But not a Reformation so
> As to reform were to o'erthrow;
> Like watches by unskilful men
> Disjointed, and set ill again.
>   (29–36)

The "Public Faith" is no better:

> The Public Faith I would adore,
> But she is bankrupt of her store;
> Nor how to trust her can I see,
> For she that cozens all, must me.
>   (37–40)

After these disappointments in a world bereft of values, the poet in the last four stanzas comes at last upon something abiding: "Since then none of these can be/Fit objects for my love and me,/ What then remains but th' only spring/Of all our loves and joys, the King?" (41–44). Having found an object of devotion, Lovelace closes with a brief prayer, with a confined Cavalier's fervent reassertion of commitment to king and cause. We recall the lines on the king in "To Althea" (cf. Horace, *Odes*, I, ii),

I
With shriller throat shall sing
The sweetness, mercy, majesty,
And glories of my king;
. . . I shall voice aloud how good
He is, how great should be
(285, 17–22),

as well as the devotion affirmed in "To Lely." The worldly Cavalier had courage and integrity when the times called for them.

Scholars, who long ascribed "To Lucasta" to the period 1648–49, regarded it as an unusually bold expression by Lovelace of his opinions of the political situation after the radical "Pride's Purge" of Parliament. H. M. Margoliouth has discovered, however, that the Kentish Petition, the presentation of which in 1642 caused Lovelace to be imprisoned, discusses the very points enumerated here. Lovelace's analysis of the state of religion, Parliament, liberty, and property is but a versification of clauses 2–7, 17, 12–13 of the petition. The "Public Faith" had at that time, moreover, become odious. Parliament often borrowed money "on the Public Faith," with little likelihood of repayment. Cowley and Cleveland attacked the bad faith of the House, and even Milton associated the term with public fraud. The poem therefore must have been written in 1642.[3]

As the political situation degenerated, the ultimate disaster of the king's execution was commemorated by the poet in a curious way. Instead of eulogizing the dead king and cause, Lovelace followed the Civil War fashion of writing versified polemics and satiric gibes in his "Mock Song." This poem is the only one of sustained irony and parody by a poet not notable for his sense of humor. It consists of mock praise of the overthrow of Charles I and the government:

Now Whitehall's in the grave,
And our head is our slave,
The bright pearl in his close shell of oyster;
Now the mitre is lost,
The proud prelates, too, crossed,
And all Rome's confin'd to a cloister;
He that Tarquin was styl'd
Our white land's exiled,
Yea undefil'd;

Not a court ape's left to confute us:
  Then let your voices rise high,
  As your colours did fly,
    And flourishing cry,
Long live the brave Oliver-Brutus!
                                    (334, 1–14)

The first stanza makes liberal use of the Parliamentary battle cries
and other clichés of the time. "Rome" is what the Anglican
Church seemed to the Puritans; the young, future Charles II was
often called Tarquin; the closing flourish utilizes the refrain of a
popular song, "O Brave Oliver."

If the first stanza is dressed in Puritan cant, the second laments
the passing of all that is significant in English society—king and
court—in a symbolism appropriate to the Royalist sentiments,
that of heraldry:

          Now the sun is unarm'd,
          And the moon by us charm'd,
        All the stars dissolv'd to a jelly;
          Now the thighs of the crown
          And the arms are lopped down,
        And the body is all but a belly:
          Let the Commons go on,
          The town is our own,
            We'll rule alone;
        For the knights have yielded their spent gorge;
          And an order is ta'en,
          With Honi Soit profane,
            Shout forth amain,
        For our Dragon hath vanquish'd the St. George.
                                    (15–28)

Willa Evans has, in "Lovelace's 'Mock Song,'" translated this
dead figurative language. The sun is a traditional symbol of the
king; the moon, of the queen. The first two lines speak therefore
of Charles I's surrendering and of Henrietta Maria's retiring to
France after being unable to reinforce Charles's troops. The stars
are the noblemen who follow the king into the dark. The "thighs
of the crown" are its chief supports, Laud and Strafford, executed
by Parliament. The lopping of the "arms" refers to the dismem-
berment of the body politic as well as to the Parliamentary order,

after the execution of Charles, to remove the royal arms from public places. "The body is all but a belly" looks back to "our head is our slave." "Let the Commons go on" alludes to the abolishment of the House of Lords, and "the town is our own" describes the Commons' control of the London officials. The knights' yielding "their spent gorge" and the profanation of "Honi Soit" indicate the extinction of the Order of the Garter, whose knights wore a collar with St. George and the dragon depicted on it. St. George's vanquishing of the dragon had become an emblem of the prosperity of England; hence the closing line summarizes the complete inversion of values, the destruction of civilization as a Royalist had understood it.

"Mock" in the title pertains not to the word "Song" but to the satirical matter of the poem—that is, a "song of mockery." These "mock songs" were one of four types of "answer poems," which, popular in the 1600–40 period, consisted of poetic rejoinders made to a poem (like, say, Marlowe's "Come, live with me") asking a question or making an assertion. The reply, in the same meter and stanza form as the original, included numerous echoes or distortions of it. Lovelace himself wrote one to Sir Thomas Wortley's "Sonnet." The "mock song" type of "answer poem" rose late, with the coming of the Civil War and the concomitant increase in polemics, invective, satire. Often caustic and intemperate, the "mock song" marks the decline of the "answer poem," which was another delicate flower of insulated court coterie life. Abuse and smut were now set to broadside ballads, or a speech was put in the mouth of an enemy. Even elegant court poets adopted a simple, crude style to reach a wide public. A ballad or parody was a relatively safe way to express Royalist outrage in Commonwealth times.[4]

For all the difficulties of the poem, readily cleared up by a knowledge of the period, Lovelace's contribution to the genre is effective and anticipates Samuel Butler's ironic "To . . . Du-Val" and mock encomia, as well as Pope's subtle, ironic needling of George II in the "Epistle to Augustus." A not overly intelligent Puritan might well have taken Lovelace's work as a pro-Parliamentary broadside. The downtrodden code of chivalry and the public values of the seventeenth-century gentleman are celebrated with clarity, specificity, ingenuity, sophistication of tone. Once again, Lovelace is at his best in expressing the Cavalier outlook.

III *Society*

Satire was not confined, however, to politics. Indeed, by tradition it dealt principally with the vices and follies of individuals, with failings of taste and manners rather than with crimes or the policies of states. Of the great themes of satire, Lovelace did not touch many. He produced only a critique of the public responses to art and poetry and a sketch of the satirist's duty in "On Sannazar's Being Honoured." Jacopo Sannazaro, an Italian poet of the late Renaissance, was awarded six hundred crowns for a six-line poem written in praise of Venice. This well-known poem was translated, or "answered," by various English writers, including Lovelace himself.

Perhaps, as Hazlitt suggested, the very act of translating the poem stimulated Lovelace to write a full-length satire. In any case, the fact that a minor poet should be rewarded so lavishly for a minor poem is used by Lovelace as grounds for an arraignment of the state of poetry and of society's disregard of quality in art. Whether Lovelace's problem or not, the plight of the starving poet elicited his interest. (It is the subject of epigrams he translated from Portius Licinus and Catullus.) Nor was this poem only a piece of literary "imitation." In "Painture," he criticized the complacent English insensitivity to the arts, its "transalpine barbarous neglect":

> Now, my best Lely, let's walk hand in hand,
> And smile at this un-understanding land;
> Let them their own dull counterfeits adore,
> Their rainbow-cloths admire, and no more;
> Within one shade of thine more substance is
> Than all their vanish'd idol-mistresses.
>   (354, 101–6)

"On Sannazar" begins with surprise at Venice's lavishness and bad taste. Lovelace contrasts the high place of the true poet in ancient Rome with his present ignominious position: Rome

> Indifferent gave to poet and to king;
> With the same laurels were his temples fraught,
> Who best had written, and who best had fought;
> The selfsame fame they equally did feel,

> One's style ador'd as much as th' other's steel.
> A chain or fasces she could then afford
> The sons of Phoebus, we, an axe or cord.
>
> (361, 26–32)

The poets of Rome formed a community, a tradition; the laurel passed from one acknowledged great writer to the next. The poet of Lovelace's day must resort to insincere devices to survive, must pander to the low taste of patron or public to receive support:

> Of princes, women, wine to sing I see
> Is no apocrypha; for, to rise high,
> Commend this olio of this lord, 'tis fit.
> There is that justice left, since you maintain
> His table, he should counterfeed your brain.
> Then write how well he in his sack hath droll'd,
> Straight there's a bottle to your chamber roll'd;
> Or with embroider'd words praise his French suit,
> Month hence 'tis yours, with his man's curse to boot;
> Or but applaud his boss'd legs, two to none
> But he most nobly doth give you one.
>
> (41–52)

The writing is brisk and amusing—note, for example, the fine wordplay in "give you one [the leg]." There are also some unwitting ironies: "Of princes, women, wine to sing" describes the bulk of Lovelace's own output; and his assertion, later, that the writing of epics is unrewarding came at the very time Milton was undertaking *Paradise Lost*.

The mock advice on advancement continues with a long, vigorous, and amusing ironic "character" of the time-serving poet who prospers by attacking the good and praising evil:

> You that do suck for thirst your black quill's blood,
> And chaw your labour'd papers for your food,
> I will inform you how and what to praise.
> Beware, as you would your fierce guests, your lice,
> To strip the cloth of gold from cherish'd Vice:
> Rather stand off with awe and reverend fear,
> Hang a poetic pendant in her ear.
> Court her as her adorers do their glass,
> Though that as much of a true substance has,

> Whilst all the gall from your wild ink you drain,
> The beauteous sweets of Virtue's cheeks you stain;
> And in your livery let her be known
> As poor and tattered as in her own.
>
>   (61–74)

The critique of the "un-understanding" patrons of culture and their lackeys turns into a portrait of those who value nothing:

> Be chaste Religion and her priests your scorn,
> Whilst the vain fanes of idiots you adorn.
> It is a mortal error, you must know,
> Of any to speak good, if he be so.
> . . . .
> Each verse be an indictment, be not free
> Sanctity 'tself from thy scurrility.
> Libel your father, and your dam buffoon,
> The noblest matrons of the isle lampoon,
> . . . .
> And in your sheets your sister prostitute.
>   (77–80, 83–86, 88)

The poet must also cater to the whims of his lady love or to the conventions which govern the writing of love poetry: To the mistress "they do all prostrate fall,/ . . . To this they sacrifice the whole day's light" (92, 95). Lovelace ridicules the hyperbole expected of the love poet and then accepts, in an ironic manner, the poet's thanks for the good advice he has offered: "Save you, bright sir,/ (O, spare your thanks) is not this finer far/Than walk unhided . . . /And your day's fare, a fortified toast" (104–6, 111).

The world of poetry has been invaded by small men who strike at great ones and bring with them violent ways and internecine war:

> Faction and envy now is downright rage.
> . . . .
> Now, as ere Nimrod the first king, he writes
> That's strongest, th' ablest deepest bites.
> The Muses weeping fly their Hill, to see
> Their noblest sons of peace in mutiny.
> Could there naught else this civil war complete,

> But poets raging with poetic heat,
> Tearing themselves and th' endless wreath.
>
> (148, 152–58)

The barbarians have overrun the realm of English poetry:

> There is not in my mind one sullen fate
> Of old, but is concentred in our state.
> Vandal o'errunners, Goths in literature,
> Ploughmen that would Parnassus new manure,
> Ringers of verse that all-in all-in chime,
> And toll the changes upon every rhyme.
> A mercer now by th' yard does measure o'er
> An ode which was but by the foot before;
> Deals you an ell of epigram, and swears
> It is the strongest, and the finest wears.
> No wonder if a drawer verses rack,
> If 'tis not his 't may be the spir't of sack;
> Whilst the fair barmaid strokes the Muse's teat,
> For milk to make the posset up complete.
> . . . .
> Behold a mist of insects. . . . .
> . . . .
> These scorpions with which we have to do
> Are fiends, not only small but deadly too.
>
> (206–19, 222, 228–29)

The theater would have put these creatures in their place: "Once a five-knotted whip there was, the Stage,/The beadle and the executioner,/To whip small errors, and the great ones tear" (149–51). But that is gone amidst the greater Civil War. Lovelace here alludes to the social satire of the Jonsonian theater. Indeed his critique, occasionally invoking good exemplars like Rome or George Sandys, now says in effect, "Jonson, thou shouldst be living at this hour!": "Arise, thou reverend shade, great Jonson, rise!" (220). We know of no tie between Jonson and Lovelace, nor does Lovelace ever call himself a "Son of Ben," as Herrick and Randolph did. Jonson nevertheless reigned over the age as the embodiment of erudition, artistic devotion, integrity, and as the *arbiter elegantiarum,* as *the* poet-playwright-critic. Reverent poems were written to him by nearly every prominent poet, including Jonson himself.

Now follows in "On Sannazar" a lively, vitriolic attack by Lovelace on women in literature:

> How would thy masc'line spirit, Father Ben,
> Sweat to behold basely deposed men
> Justled from the prerog'tive of their bed,
> Whilst wives are per'wigg'd with their husband's head!
> Each snatches the male quill from his faint hand,
> And must both nobler write and understand,
> He to her fury the soft plume doth bow:
> O pen! ne'er truly justly slit till now!
> Now as herself a poem she doth dress,
> And curls a line as she would do a tress;
> Powders a sonnet as she does her hair,
> Then prostitutes them both to public air.
> Nor is 't enough that they their faces blind
> With a false dye, but they must paint their mind;
> In metre scold, and in scann'd order brawl.
>   (234–48)

The attack on these unidentified women is partly an "imitation" of a Classical model, Juvenal's sixth satire. To Lovelace, citing Jonson was apropos since he had, in the *Masque of the Metamorphosed Gipsies,* expressed a dislike of women and their aspirations to power.

Having reached a climax of vituperation, Lovelace closes the poem calmly by returning to the starting point—the Clarrissimi of Venice and Sannazar. He drops his ire and his ironic praise of evil:

> Forgive what thus distemper'd I indite,
> For it is hard a satire not to write.
> Yet as a virgin that heats all her blood
> At the first motion of bad understood,
> Then at mere thought of fair chastity,
> Straight cools again the tempests of her sea:
>   So, when to you I my devotions raise,
>   *All wrath and storms do end in calms and praise.*
>   (260–67)

Though unknown to any but the scholar, this longest of Lovelace poems and the only one labeled a "satire" contains some of his finest lines and suggests that, had he survived into the Restoration, he might have made some important contributions to its literature. If the meter, the subject matter, the frank criticism, and the bitter tone seem unlike the genteel Lovelace we know, our reaction merely bespeaks the limitations of the Lovelace of our own making. If the theme of woman's domination of literature hardly seems a major problem of the Commonwealth years, and if the theme of the poet's dependence on patrons does not reflect a personal difficulty of Lovelace's, who was more likely to have been a patron of poets (at least in his earlier years) than to have sought one, their presence may be due to the examples of Juvenal's Satires I (on bad poets and the vile society that adopts them and makes satire necessary), VII (on the misery and poverty of the intellectual life), VI (on the tyranny of wives, the rule of strong-willed women in politics and poetry), which Lovelace's work imitates. Though there are few specific parallels—such as the famous line "it is hard a satire not to write"—the indirect influences abound; and the poem is long enough and sufficiently broad in scope to come within the category of Juvenalian satire.[5]

Satire was normally written in rough measures and with cryptic allusions. Lovelace's poem has a randomness and its quota of obscure or lifeless passages, but it often rises above them. Written in heroic couplets rather than in Lovelace's usual stanzaic forms, it is a link in the chain of English Horatian and Juvenalian satires that begins with Marston, Joseph Hall, and especially the forceful Donne, and that leads, through the obscure ones of Lord Herbert, the verbal fireworks of Cleveland, and the coarse but pioneering work of Marvell and Oldham, to the triumphs of Dryden and the elegance of Pope.

CHAPTER 5

"Love Enthroned": Courtly Love Lyrics

BY FAR the greatest part of Lovelace's poetry is about love—
an imbalance that exists in the work of quite a few poets of
the period. To understand that emphasis, we must consider briefly
the history of the amatory lyric. Great love poetry, first written by
Sappho and the Latin elegists, was resuscitated and given a new
direction in the twelfth century by the Troubadors of the Provence and the Minnesingers of Germany. Their devotion to the
lady and to their own amatory passion begot a kind of religion of
love, which has come to be known as the "courtly love tradition."
The important new idea was that love ennobles its victims. The
man in love, spurred by his passion to be worthy of his lady, becomes the paragon of courtesy and champion of his beloved; he
takes on challenges, enters tourneys, and undergoes adventures
full of risks; he establishes his submissiveness to the lady by his
prowess and courage in confronting the world.

The single most influential love poet was Petrarch (1304–74).
He married the sonnet form to love poetry, writing some three
hundred examples of it; he, more than Dante, popularized the
gesture of devoting a large sonnet sequence to the lady—while
she lived and after she died—with the dim outline of a story discernible in it. Petrarch developed an imagery, a hyperbole, and a
rhetoric which were to become standard for expressing the effects
of love. The Petrarchan style consisted of paradoxes and oxymora
("I burn! I freeze!"); of exaggerated images, such as of floods
caused by the unrequited lover's tears and windstorms caused by
his sighs; of puns and wordplay on names, especially the lady's;
and of certain stock situations, like the contrast between burgeon-
ing spring and the melancholy lover. In England, though Petrarch
was translated by Wyatt and Surrey in the 1530's, the full impact
of Petrarchism came in the last decade of the sixteenth century,

when nearly every writer with any pretensions to poetry wrote a sonnet sequence.

At the dawn of the seventeenth century, the Troubadors of Provence had slipped from view; but the sonnets of Petrarch and his Italian and French followers were carefully read. The Renaissance code of the gentleman placed great emphasis on the heuristic value of the love experience. Even someone like Ben Jonson, who deliberately eschewed the fashionable Petrarchan imagery and sonnet form, modeled himself on the polished, detached love poetry of the late Greeks and the Romans, which as a result of the rediscovery of antiquity, was as never before a cultural presence. John Donne, the other great poet who refrained from joining the sonneteering avalanche, composed a series of equally unsentimental, even cynical, love poems that are reminiscent somewhat of Ovid. In other lyrics, Donne was capable of exalted expressions of tenderness. In range, variety, style, he was immensely influential on the English poets of the next two generations. His influence is manifested in, for example, the divorce of the long-wedded love and sonnet traditions and in the variety of Lovelace's amatory poetry, a variety greater than in the work of any other poet of the century. But the quality of Lovelace's work, to be sure, falls far short of Donne's.

I   *The Possessed Lover*

Of Lovelace's poems, one large group, which may be loosely called "Petrarchan," conventionally delineates the plight of the unrequited lover and celebrates the lady. What this situation involves is described satirically by Lovelace in one of his more detached, jaundiced moments:

> There is a creature (if I may so call
> That unto which they do all prostrate fall)
> Term'd mistress, when they're angry, but pleas'd high,
> It is a princess, saint, divinity.
> To this they sacrifice the whole day's light,
> Then lie with their devotion all night:
> For this you are to dive to the Abyss,
> And rob for pearl the closet of some fish.
> Arabia and Sabaea you must strip
> Of all their sweets, for to supply her lip.
>
> (362, 91–100)

The lover observes the lady, desires her, and is fired by his passion. Her capriciousness generates conflicting emotions in him: "Now broil'd i' th' zone of her reflected light,/Then froze, my icicles not sinews shake" (315, 18–19). Night is turned into a torture:

> Like to the sent'nel stars, I watch all night;
> For still the grand round of your light,
>   And glorious breast,
>   Awakes in me an east,
> Nor will my rolling eyes e'er know a west.
>
> Now on my down I'm toss'd as on a wave,
> And my repose is made my grave.
>   (318, 1–7)

When "captive Day his chariot mounted is;/Night to her proper hell is beat" (314, 11–12), and the freezing and broiling continue without a break; "bondslave I know neither day nor night" (16). He grows hypersensitive and is subject to rapid changes of moods: "I laugh and sing . . . /But then I groan/ . . . Love does this" (318, 1, 3, 7).

Indeed, the lady does it. She is sadistic; the lover's tears beget but her laughter:

>   She laughs again
>   At our ridiculous pain;
>   And at our merry misery
>   She laughs until she cry.
>
>   . . . .
> That which still makes her mirth to flow
> Is our sinister-handed woe.
>   (312, 6–9, 14–15)

He is completely dehumanized by the terrible experience: "In mine own monument I lie,/And in myself am buried;/Sure the quick lightning of her eye/Melted my soul i' th' scabbard dead" (330, 1–4); but he is also ambivalent: "This is such a pleasing pain,/I'm loth to be alive again" (11–12). Besides, "it is the glory of a valiant lover/Still to be dying, still for to recover" (260, 11–12).

The lover would like to be put out of his misery: "Pity me no more,/Or else more pity me" (297, 1–2). His debacle is caused by his uncertainty; he is neither outrightly rejected nor favored with her attentions. By pitying him, she could relieve his misery in the way he would prefer; but, if she cannot do so, at least by turning completely away from him, she would free his emotions from their bondage, "For left thus as I am,/My heart is ice and flame;/ And languishing thus I/Can neither live nor die!" (297, 5–8).

Although in the poetry of the courtly love tradition, the love relationship is considered almost exclusively from the point of view of the man, the woman is allowed to speak in a few instances. When Lovelace presents in two poems the woman's side, he uses, curiously enough, the dramatic monologue in rhyming couplets instead of the usual stanzaic lyric. In "Against the Love of Great Ones," a high-born lady tells of the folly of the young man in love with one like her, who will have nothing to do with *hoi polloi:* "Unhappy youth, betray'd by fate/To such a love hath sainted hate,/ . . . /The love of great ones. 'Tis a love/Gods are incapable to prove" (282, 1–2, 5–6). Andreas Capellanus, the medieval high priest of courtly love, had stated that love can, within limits, cut across class barriers; but this lady is suspicious of the youth's motivation: has he fallen for her wealth, or rank, or body, or character?

> What is it that you would possess,
> The countess, or the naked Bess?
> Would you her gown or title do,
> Her box, or gem, her thing or show?
> If you mean her, the very her
> Abstracted from her character,
> Unhappy boy! you may as soon
> With fawning wanton with the moon,
> Or with an amorous complaint
> Get prostitute your very saint.
>   (31–40)

The lady's hauteur springs from a proper sense of her high origins, not from frigidity:

> Not that we are not mortal, or
> Fly Venus' altars, or abhor

> The selfsame knack for which you pine;
> But we (defend us!) are divine,
> Female, but madam born, and come
> From a right-honourable womb:
> Shall we then mingle with the base,
> And bring a silver-tinsel race?
>
> (41–48)

Even though she will not have anything serious to do with such
young men, she enjoys playing with and torturing them. In this
respect she is like Lucasta and the other unrequiting ladies; her
class pride merely makes the Petrarchan lover's plight the more
hopeless.

In "A Forsaken Lady," not only is the woman herself the victim
of unrequited love; the object of her passion has become infected
with a like disease. The man, caught between the rejected woman
who wants him and the attractive woman who does not, is addressed by the former in a mixture of tender concern—she would
like to assuage his torments—and *schadenfreude* at his being re-
paid in kind:

> Uncharitablest both ways, to deny
> That pity me, for which yourself must die,
> To love not her loves you, yet know the pain
> What 'tis to love and not be lov'd again.
>
> (257, 15–18)

The image proper to their mutual distress is of running, fleeing:

> Fly on, fly on, swift racer,
>
> . . . .
>   Not yet look back, nor yet; must we
> Run then like spokes in wheels eternally,
> And never overtake? . . . No, I will turn,
> And with my goodness boldly meet your scorn.
>
> (19, 23–28)

She changes her mind; she will reciprocate his bitter scorn. Iron
has entered her soul, and she will be indifferent to him: "Hail,
holy cold! chaste temper, hail! the fire/Rav'd o'er my purer
thoughts I feel t' expire,/And I am candi'd ice" (39–41). She thus
becomes the Petrarchan lady, remote and untouchable.

II *The Lady's Attractiveness*

The Petrarchan lover is not alone in being so deeply affected;
the lady's physical attractions are strong enough to bestir also the
natural world. The falcon, though "princess of the air," is made
submissive; the bee is drawn to her face and willingly dies there:
"Near both her suns he makes his bed/ . . . /And in these holy
flames doth glad expire" (317, 7, 19). The pathetic fallacy of nature's response to the lady's beauty is most fully developed in the
pastoral, "Aramantha." The heifers present themselves to her,
"begging her charitable leisure/To strip them of their milky treasure" (305, 87–88); the fish without bait or angle is a "happy captive, gladly ta'en,/[and] Sues ever to be slave in vain" (143–44);
farther in the woods, she is serenaded by the "winged music of the
air." The very flowers vibrate to her presence as the heroine enters
the garden:

> And freely to her lap proscribe
> A daughter out of ev'ry tribe:
>
> . . . .
>   The noble heliotropion
> Now turns to her, and knows no sun.
>
> . . . .
> So all their due obedience pay,
> Each thronging to be in her way.
>   (304, 49–50, 53–54, 77–78)

The propinquity of beautiful woman and flower is etched most
nicely in "The Rose." The poet builds to a climax wherein the
flower, like the princess falcon, is suddenly diminished vis-à-vis
the beloved: "But early as she dresses,/Why fly you her bright
tresses?/Ah! I have found I fear:/Because her cheeks are near"
(249, 21–24). The rose often appears in Renaissance love poetry
as a symbol of the lady's beauty or of its transience, but rarely has
the idea of the roselike beauty of her cheeks been expressed so
deftly.

Even inanimate objects respond to such beauty: "Behold how
lightning like a taper flies,/And gilds your chari't, but ashamed
dies,/Seeing itself outglori'd by your eyes" (302, 10–12). In "The
Guiltless Lady Imprisoned," the things which confine the lady are
transformed by her: the gyves "play about thy wanton wrist/As if

in them thou so wert dress'd;/But if too rough, too hard they press,/Oh they but closely, closely kiss" (288, 13–16).

The lady's beauty is often immortalized on canvas, and the poet celebrates that event, as in "Upon the Curtain of Lucasta's Picture." But beauty of some sort there must be if the poet is to be moved; for among the various poems praising the lady's attractiveness are two which declare, in what we would consider an unchivalrous manner, his independence from the lady because she lacks charm. In "When I," the cause of the difficulty is the lady's inconsiderate fickleness in allowing herself to age. In "You Are Deceived," the vituperation becomes direct and insulting; he cannot write about a lady who is ugly; the poet's humble role is to extol the beauty found in life: "It is just Heaven on beauty stamps a fame,/And we, alas! its triumphs but proclaim" (331, 9–10). If he were to laud anything else, he would be lowering standards and in effect insulting the praiseworthy beautiful. Attempting to soothe her feelings, he approaches the matter more considerately from her point of view. By writing of her, he would actually be drawing attention to her and arousing in others expectations she could not fulfill; her charmlessness would thereby be exposed:

> 'Twere better, heavy one, to crawl
> Forgot, than, raised, trod on fall:
>   All your defections now
>   Are not writ on your brow.
>   Odes to faults give
>   A shame must live.
>
> (23–28)

He concludes matter of factly with the brutal truth: "For since thy birth gave thee no beauty, know/No poet's pencil must or can do so" (39–40). Since poets often claim to be moved to composition and inspired in felicitous esthetic decisions by the beloved's beauty, such a blunt, harsh indictment of the lady's ugliness is, although tactless, consistent. The theme is Classical (cf. Horace's *Epodes* viii, xii and Martial, VII, lxxv) and expressed with a verve; the poem's diction and metrics have been praised by several critics.

The lady's physical charms do not exist discretely but are held together by a certain way of doing things. A woman with lovely features and gawky comportment is unattractive. But beauty of character, like beauty of body or bearing, is in the beholder's eye. And, once the man is enamored of the lady, all things related to her, anything her body touches or that she shows interest in, become galvanized in the eyes of the man. Hence the series of poems which lavish attention on some of her possessions springs from a literary tradition no less than from emotions natural to all lovers. There is, for instance, Catullus' famous poem on Lesbia's sparrow or Meleager's wish that he were the wine cup touched by the lady's lips. Petrarch wrote poems on such things as Laura's glove, and Romeo exclaims, "O that I were a glove upon that hand,/That I might touch that cheek!"

Even humble articles are envied or become the subject of the poet's wit and ingenuity. The lady's fan being made of ostrich feathers, the bird is described as "transformed into a bird of paradise" (266, 5–8). The lady's muff represents her power over the animal kingdom: "Beasts to thee a sacrifice . . . bleed,/And strip themselves to make you gay" (316, 17–18). Even a patch on the lady's face can be turned to good account. "A Black Patch," we saw, constructs a little myth to account for the object; in another poem with the same title, the poet avails himself of the old Petrarchan comparison of his lady to the sun: The patch is a cloud:

> Behold Lucasta's face, how 't glows like noon!
> A sun entire is her complexion,
> And form'd of one whole constellation.
>
> So gently shining, so serene, so clear,
> Her look doth universal Nature cheer;
> Only a cloud or two hangs here and there.
> (318, 16–21)

The best of the poems on the lady's possessions is "Ellinda's Glove." The poet calls on the lady, but she is out. He finds her glove left behind:

> Thou snowy farm with thy five tenements!
>   Tell thy white mistress here was one
>   That call'd to pay his daily rents;
> But she a-gathering flow'rs and hearts is gone,
> And thou left void to rude possession.
> (270, 1–5)

Nearly each line here carries a conceit in Lovelace's usual manner, but for once each conceit seems apt: the white glove as a snowy farmhouse with five apartments now unoccupied; the caller as both a tenant paying rent and as a suitor; the mistress away gathering flowers and hearts—smiting other men. In the second stanza, the image changes. The glove has become a cabinet into which only the lady's hand can fit, so special is she:

> But grieve not, pretty ermine cabinet,
>   Thy alabaster lady will come home;
>   If not, what tenant can there fit
> The slender turnings of thy narrow room,
> But must ejected be by his own doom?
>   (6–10)

The last stanza returns to the initial image of the poet as tenant; then the imagery abruptly shifts again: the lover takes the liberty of touching and kissing the glove without being free to do the like to the lady, just as a servant, without knowing the art of playing the lute, may handle the outer case:

> Then give me leave to leave my rent with thee:
>   Five kisses, one unto a place;
>   For though the lute's too high for me,
> Yet servants knowing minikin [= lute pin] nor base
> Are still allow'd to fiddle with the case.
>   (11–15)

The kisses he leaves are proper to both his roles here, as lover and as tenant paying his rent.

This lovely little poem has been a touchstone of taste. Its playful tone proved a stumbling block to those who, operating under the Victorian "high seriousness" fallacy, looked for "sincerity," "depth of feeling." Thus Edmund Gosse, repelled by the conceits, took the trouble to analyze the structure of the lyric in order to disclose its alleged randomness and lack of unity. He found it remarkable even in an age of "concetti" for its "tasteless fancy," its dwelling—in typical Lovelace extravagance—on the periphery of the subject, and its insipid imitation of the Donne fashion. To the twentieth-century mind, the mental acrobatics which annoyed Gosse make the poem alive. Instead of randomness and extravagance, we see a nimble mind readily finding apt analogies in conveying what it feels like to be, on the one hand, disappointed by the absence of a lady one comes to visit and, on the other hand, cheered by the presence of an object associated with her. George Williamson compares the lyric, in richness of conceit, to Donne's "Flea"; A. C. Baugh calls it the prettiest of Lovelace's lesser works; and Geoffrey Walton thinks it nothing less than brilliant.[1]

As imposing as the personal beauty and possessions are the lady's gestures and actions. The humblest of these can be, if performed by the lady-love, transmuted by the man's elixir-like infatuation. As Yeats put it, one loves a woman not because she is beautiful or intelligent but because of the way she scratches her hair. The lover readily takes joy in observing his lady in motion. She may, in the midst of her falconry, suddenly loom as mistress of all. Surrounded by men, as in "Lucasta's World," her every sigh and smile makes its impact. Men are also tremulous witnesses of her singing and dancing, as in "Gratiana Dancing and Singing":

> See! with what constant motion,
> Even and glorious as the sun,
>   Gratiana steers that noble frame,
> Soft as her breast, sweet as her voice
> That gave each winding law and poise,
>   And swifter than the wings of Fame.
>
> She beat the happy pavement
> By such a star made firmament,
>   Which now no more the roof envies,
> But swells up high with Atlas ev'n,
> Bearing the brighter, nobler heav'n,
>   And, in her, all the deities.
>
> Each step trod out a lover's thought
> And the ambitious hopes he brought,
>   Chain'd to her brave feet with such arts,
> Such sweet command and gentle awe,
> As when she ceas'd, we sighing saw
>   The floor lay pav'd with broken hearts.
>   (250, 1–18)

As in "Ellinda's Glove," the imagery of this poem changes rapidly. Her presence changes the floor into a firmament; she in turn becomes a heaven on it; the floor then is transformed from a heaven with one shining star into a floor paved with broken hearts.

This poem has also found its champions mainly in the twentieth century. An old-fashioned critic, Oliver Elton, found it a fanciful lyric with little humor; but Grierson and Bullough think that the ingenious third stanza at least expresses perfectly the feeling that "to love and to be wise is given to no man." To Douglas Bush, the poem is a radiant Elizabethan vision oscillating between naïveté and fantastic sophistication. Hollander regards it a well-turned lyric rising above the convention it is a part of, and Walton enjoys the large-scale conceit and the subtle rhythm. R. C. Bald calls it "really original and justly famous," while James Reeves, admiring the extravagant metaphor typical of Lovelace, finds this poem better even than the two famous ones, "To Althea" and "To Lucasta." [2]

Since love and music were often cited by Renaissance writers as forms of harmony, complimentary epigrams on the affective power of the lady's dancing or singing are numberless. The one action appeals to the eye, the other to the ear, and both harmonies —frequently related to the music of the spheres—also pleased conjointly. Likewise current are poems of the lady weeping. Lovelace's own "Lucasta Weeping" and "Lucasta Paying Her Obsequis," however, are lifeless. Another common posture for the lady is self-observation in a mirror. Poems in this genre oscillate between decrying the lady's narcissistic tendencies and expressing envy of the mirror. Lovelace's version, "Lucasta's Fan," has a happy ending. An equally characteristic action is the lady's immersion in the baths of a fashionable spa. In "Lucasta Taking the Waters at Tunbridge," the poet envies the waters blessed by their contact with her body. "Ye happy floods! that now must pass/The sacred conduits of her womb" (267, 1–2). In the later "Lucasta at the Bath," she is compared to a ship; wind and water are powerless before her.

III Lovers' Parting

The most critical of the lady's actions is to leave the man. The tender, temporary parting of the lovers, one of Donne's great themes, is the subject of several Lovelace lyrics. In the "Dialogue" between Lucasta and Alexis, the woman is vexed, while the man characteristically minimizes the event. Unlike the more famous separation poems, in which the man's thoughts are central, this dialogue is a debate on the question of whether love can be expected to survive physical separation. Alexis' various affirmative arguments are hardly heard by the distraught Lucasta, who speaks of man's forgetfulness, of her devotion to Alexis, and of her wish to dream of him, be with him, forever.

The theme of parting is more excitingly handled in "Song. To Lucasta, going beyond the Seas," the first poem in the 1649 collection:

> If to be absent were to be
>   Away from thee;
>   Or that when I am gone
>   You or I were alone;
> Then, my Lucasta, might I crave
> Pity from blust'ring wind, or swallowing wave.
>
> But I'll not sigh one blast or gale
>   To swell my sail,
>   Or pay a tear to swage
>   The foaming blue god's rage;
> For whether he will let me pass
> Or no, I'm still as happy as I was.
>
> Though seas and land betwixt us both,
>   Our faith and troth,
>   Like separate souls,
>   All time and space controls:
> Above the highest sphere we meet
> Unseen, unknown, and greet as angels greet.
>
> So then we do anticipate,
>   Our after-fate,
>   And are alive i' th' skies,
>   If thus our lips and eyes
> Can speak like spirits unconfin'd
> In heav'n, their earthly bodies left behind.
>
> (245)

In this poem the parting is seen through the eyes of the lover only. Instead of debate, we have the evocation of a mood: the confidence that the lovers will not be alone despite absence, that souls have an angel-like capacity to achieve an ethereal existence without the bodies. The poem is heavily influenced by Donne; but, though it lacks the master's fireworks, Lovelace shows sufficient poetic dexterity of his own: the tight logical structure, the intense lyric quality, and the deft use of short and long lines. C. V. Wedgwood cites, for the magical rightness of sound, the opening "breathless run of short vowels" followed by the yearning emphasis of the two long vowels in the second line. Indeed, critical comment has been ample on this perfect lyric.[3]

The theme of parting is treated consummately in the poem which immediately follows, "Song. To Lucasta, going to the Wars":

> Tell me not, sweet, I am unkind,
>   That from the nunnery
> Of thy chaste breast and quiet mind,
>   To war and arms I fly.
>
> True, a new mistress I now chase,
>   The first foe in the field;
> And with a stronger faith embrace
>   A sword, a horse, a shield.
>
> Yet this inconstancy is such
>   As you too shall adore;
> I could not love thee, dear, so much
>   Lov'd I not Honour more.
>
>   (246)

With "To Althea," this poem—"one of the briefest masterpieces in the world," according to Mark Van Doren—is the only one by Lovelace known to everyone who reads any poetry at all. Its triumph is the greater in that it consists of twelve brief lines in which the poet uses the simplest language, imagery, logical structure. The last two lines, in particular, are so famous because they cannot be paraphrased and are therefore the best proof, as Van Doren adds, that poetry can say what nothing else can. A good line of poetry is the shortest distance between two points, and the present two points—nunnery and battlefield—are worlds apart.[4]

As in the best of Donne or Marvell, the lover of this poem addresses his lady in a dramatic scene we can readily visualize.

About to leave her, he takes his farewell and assuages her grief.
Though only he speaks, her feelings are expressed by his ambiguous, potentially self-accusatory words. In the first stanza, as in the
first of "To . . . Seas," he forestalls an argument by passively
stating or restating Lucasta's complaint. In the second stanza, he
yields a point only to force her to yield the entire argument in the
last. In the second stanza he sees himself as free of the lady and as
aggressively re-establishing his identity in an active world, and
the language in this stanza is hyperbolic, clever; ideas rather than
feelings are at work, as is consistent with the tone of persuasion,
which reaches for paradox and exaggeration. In what seems at first
a concession to her likely suspicion and anger, he uses the language of the love triangle, "a new mistress," "inconstancy." He is
being ironic, however, and merely setting the stage for a turnabout in which he will obtain her acquiescence by showing a consistency in his role as lover.

In the third stanza, he proclaims his viewpoint as triumphant.
What calls him away is no "other woman" nor even a shifted allegiance or a new sort of love, such as of war; what beckons is
something she also must admire. He is running *to* something—
honor—not *from* her. He is not merely doing his duty; he "loves"
honor and that love is not anything new, competitive, or distract-
ing. Returning in the third stanza to the use of the second person
and to the feelings of the first stanza, he re-emphasizes the
lady's chastity by citing her adoration of honor. "Sweet" in line
one, set off by commas, as if accompanied tenderly by a vow, a
kiss, a wiping away of a tear, has become "dear" in line eleven.
The word "dear," a final assessment not only of quality but also of
value, suggests that she indicates agreement by a brightening fa-
cial expression, as she joins him in the higher, more spiritual love.
"Sweet" intimates enjoyment of the lady, but "dear" connotes esteem, respect.

The prosody, ably analyzed by Van Doren and Norman Holland, is subtle. The first stanza's many long "i" sounds and slow
phrases establish the atmosphere of tranquility, respect, chastity,
and the affection with which the lover treats Lucasta. Before we
rush to line three for the syntax, we are forced to linger on the last
syllable of "nunnery" to make it rhyme; the balance of thrusts
nicely suggests reluctance, hesitation. The next line consists of
slow monosyllables evoking serenity, while line four is quick, with

harsh alien words. The rest of the poem is, as it were, spoken over his shoulder by the departing lover; the music of lines two and three is never entirely recaptured. The second stanza is notably filled with "s" 's, "t" 's, "th" 's, stout "f" 's, which conjure up aggressiveness and hostility.[5]

G. F. Jones has examined the meaning of the all-important word, "honor." The *Oxford English Dictionary*, citing this poem, defines it as integrity, an inner rightness in contradistinction to feelings of guilt and sin. This sense is the modern, subjective one, but Jones concludes that the older, objective meaning—of good name, reputation, "image"—is intended, as in the rest of Lovelace's work and in all earlier literature. Jones ties this poem to a venerable literary tradition depicting the conflict between shame caused by loss of face as a warrior, and love. Citing works from the Greek, Roman, and Germanic traditions, Jones asserts that this lyric dramatizes the old dilemma of the warrior having to choose between love with shame and action with glory, as in Corneille's *Cid*—"un homme sans honneur ne te meritait [a man without honor is not worthy of you]." To buttress his point, Jones notes archaisms in the poem like "shield"—an implement proper to the Middle Ages and no longer used in the seventeenth century.[6]

The vocations of the lover and the warrior have indeed long been venerated as two supreme masculine activities. They are mutually dependent, and when Othello's role as a lover and husband dissolves, his career as general—his "occupation"—ends too. But sometimes, as ancient writers like Propertius, Ovid, Horace intimated, the two disciplines clash. In *Antony and Cleopatra*, the hero is undone by their rival claims. Lovelace's own "To Lucasta. From Prison" presents the poet turning from love to a renewal of his allegiance to king.

"To war and arms" (echoing Virgil's *arma virumque*), "foe," "sword," "horse," "shield" conjure up the glories of battle and chivalry. "Mistress" and "love" bespeak the other vocation—not the turbulent passion of courtly or promiscuous love, but the "nunnery" of "chaste breast and quiet mind." There is, therefore, besides the contrast between Lucasta and war, love and honor, one between the serenity of love and the turbulence of the outside world to which the man must now turn. In a sense this poem, especially the first stanza, is but another version of the old dichotomy of the active and contemplative lives, with love taking the place of studies as the core of contemplation.

The basic conflict is resolved as the lover forces the lady to accede to his departure by showing his actions to be consistent with fidelity and with her values. The last two lines, so well known independently and so beautiful in their epigrammatic quality, have an important function in the argument of the poem. Easing departure by avoiding sentimentality, they present a paradox. She is not only asked to suppress charges of inconstancy and to put aside suspicions; she is made to see that his very love for her rests on the concept of honor that both share. By "inconstancy," he means "alleged" or "so-called" inconstancy; for this other love accords with his present one.

The theme of this poem can thus be regarded as antithetical to the theme of *Antony and Cleopatra:* to be a true lover, the man must at the same time retain his other vocation, his martial honor. In Western love, at least—no doubt because of the family structure, in which the male is breadwinner—the woman need only be her attractive and virtuous self, but the lover has had by tradition to be something else; his quality as lover has rested on his proficiency in some alien discipline. This concept of honor as a prerequisite of love is a heritage of the courtly love tradition, which in a sense was a reaction to the older view of the conflict of Venus and Mars. The lover's heeding the call of honor is like the medieval knight undertaking difficult tasks imposed on him by his lady love to prove his quality and the depth of his devotion. In Lovelace's poem, the task is imposed by public events and by the lover's conscience rather than by the lady, who has to be reminded of the ennobling and self-sacrificing requirements of love, who has to be shown what she would desire of her own volition if she but knew or remembered.

Without this mastery, this honor, the lover is not worthy of the lady; he has not the capacity or merit to love. To love properly, he must be more devoted to honor. If he cannot have, according to the Renaissance's heritage of the courtly love tradition and Neo-Platonism, honor without experiencing love, neither can he merit love without having honor. Were he to stay behind when duty and loyalty called him, he would lose not only honor but also thereby her love, whether she admitted it or not. She must therefore respect such "inconstancy." Her love of honor, we are to understand, makes him love her, even as his love of honor over love of woman makes her love him, makes him worthy of her love.

Only she could adore what he does because she is so special. In Van Doren's paraphrase, "I love honor more, and you have helped me to do so, because you love it as much as you do." Her worship of honor educates him. Mutual adoration of honor is bigger than both of them, and it is a bond between them which overcomes separation and paradoxically makes their love possible. As N. H. Pearson points out, Lovelace pays her the supreme compliment of openly avowing his love of honor and its inherent superiority to his relationship with her. The seeming unkindness of his leaving her is but an illusion of fleshly existence—an illusion removed in the last stanza. "Nunnery" in the first stanza indicates the sanctified refuge the mistress provided and suggests that their union consists of one indivisible spirit rather than of two separable bodies. The religious overtones of "adore" and "honor" in the third stanza remind us of "nunnery," for "honor" means not only his soldierly good name and virile aggressiveness but also her chastity.

The last stanza, therefore, establishes the idea of continuity amid change, as Pearson suggests; though the lover leaves her, their affection persists. His departure is not what it at first seems, an abandonment, but a result of their shared values—"You too. . . ." The lover, Van Doren observes, is not lamenting the necessity of leaving but is justifying it, even exulting in it. The opening imperative sentence gives a sense of authority as well as gentleness to his words, for he expects her to understand. The appeal to honor, according to H. M. Richmond, also frees the lady of apprehension over her lover's abandoning her. If he leaves to risk death on behalf of a principle or king, he is not likely to fail challenges to the comparable principle of loyalty to her. The lover does not justify his flight so much as certify that he will return to her. Or, to put it conversely, were he to value his lady more than his honor, he might someday deal with her with less than honor.[7]

This poem is a memorable product of the English Civil War. Juxtaposing it with Carew's "Rapture," Suckling's "Why so," or even Lovelace's own erotica reminds us that Cavalier poetry had its opposite poles; that, in fact, this clear call to honor was rare in seventeenth-century literature, despite all of the rhetoric thrown

up by the conflicting sides. Most appeals to honor tend to be in-
flated, to sound like moral cant. This one does not.

Moreover, this is a love poem which transcends the genre by
making love less important; it is a poem of parting which with-
holds the usual consolations of visits via dreams or imminent reunion; a war poem which deals not with issues or political ideas
but with the way in which war affects human relationships. Here
the poetry of courtly love, by redefining love, reaches beyond itself. The poem expresses what most men feel or would like to be
able to feel in such a situation; it puts perfectly what is a valid and
beautiful outlook, an ideal of manly conduct. Though it, with "To
Althea," is the supreme document of the Cavalier spirit in its presentation of the aristocratic dilemma between love and honor and
in its dramatization of the change in the Cavalier milieu from the
insulated court life and loves of the 1630's to the turmoil of the
1640's, it speaks of a universal situation that confronts every man
at some time and in some way.

This lyric is intimately connected with two other famous Lovelace poems. Holland draws an interesting comparison with "The
Scrutiny," in which a lover also feels like a possessed, passive captive and also talks his lady into letting him leave; there too the
lover looks to a re-establishment of his identity through renewed
aggressive contact with the world and to an ultimate resolution, a
reconciliation of a sort with the lady. But, though the form is similar, the content is different. The lover of "To . . . Wars" appeals
to the shared value of "honor," while the lover of "Scrutiny" appeals to a concept of "variety" which he must first impart to the
lady. Both poems, moreover, rest on a Platonic assumption; for
the lovers suggest, seriously in "Wars" and mockingly in "Scrutiny," that love is not static, not constant to any earthly object.
The lady is a springboard to something higher; in "Wars," the
man ascends the ladder of love from love of her to love of honor.[8]

Verbal parallels also unite Lovelace's two most famous lyrics,
"To Althea" and "Wars": "*Minds innocent* and *quiet* take/That
for an *hermitage*" and "the *nunnery*/Of thy *chaste* breast and
quiet mind." The one poem celebrates the persistence of the joyful
love of life amid confinement; the other, the resolution of a universal dilemma by a proper gradation of values. The prisoner,
content with his love and with the state of his soul, readily accepts
the burden of physical confinement; the lover, content with his

love, readily accepts the burden laid upon him by duty and honor
to leave her and join the fray. In either case, the man's serenity
enables him to endure whatever fate presents to him, whatever his
other great vocation of warrior demands of him—loyalty in confinement, separation from love. The prisoner can remain free
though shackled, perhaps most free as a result of that very confinement; the lovers can be together despite bodily separation. In
both poems, the mind, the proper attitude, overcomes the dis-
tresses of isolation caused by confinement or separation. Both
poems are about the forging of unity of being, at-oneness, in the
crucible of adversity, experience, tension. Both celebrate man's
dignity through the triumph of spirit over flesh.

CHAPTER 6

"Naked in their Bliss": Erotic Love Lyrics

I *John Donne and Don John*

THE general reader categorizes Lovelace with Sir John Suckling as debonair Cavaliers whose dandyish ways, blended with intense loyalty to Charles I, were the mirrors of fashion. As love poets, it is further assumed, they divided fields of specialization between them: Suckling composed flippant, libertine verses; Lovelace wrote about courtly, genteel love and ideal Cavalier sentiments.

Such simplistic contrasts in black and white rarely sustain investigation. The generally racy nature of much of Suckling's poetry is undeniable; but not so well known is the fact that Lovelace also wrote quite a few poems which, though not as gross as Suckling's "Candle," would cause an embarrassed stir in polite society. Lovelace, the poet of "honor," could attack and deride it in drink and seduction lyrics. The existence of this other, cynical, skeptical side of Lovelace prompted Emile Legouis to observe that Richardson was justified in using "Lovelace" as the name of the villain in *Clarissa;* but what the seventeenth century understood by the words "gentleman" and "Cavalier" was unlike our half-Victorian definitions. The truth is that Lovelace and Suckling share much in common in outlook and output; only when writing their best things do they veer in different directions.

We must not be led by the previous chapter's sketch of the history of the love lyric into thinking that only pure, ennobling love was celebrated. All countries and ages have had realistic concepts about the ways of a lad with a lass, and poetry bore witness to that view. In England, the seamy underside of amatory relations was depicted in lyric verse with intensity, candor, and verisimilitude perhaps for the first time by John Donne. His libertine works made a profound impression on the seventeenth century, principally on poets of the 1630's and 1640's. The existence of a Donne school writing "hard" poetry of libertinism and cynicism is due not

only to the excellent examples composed by the master but also to
the *Zeitgeist*. The waves of Petrarchan love pleading and idealiza-
tion of woman naturally begot a reaction. This poetry of revulsion
and revolt died down after the Restoration, concurrently with the
decline of courtly amatory verse. The worldly, cynical poems of
Lovelace are, therefore, to be seen as taking their place in the line,
spanning some eighty years, from Donne to Rochester.

In one group of poems, Lovelace justifies sexual promiscuity
with all the resources of logic used by Donne in such poems as
"The Indifferent" and "Communitie." In Lovelace's "A Paradox,"
the lover, when confronted with the observation that his previous
mistress had been more attractive than his current one, replies by
citing the difference between steady, stagnant pleasure and volup-
tuous intensity, and by advancing quasi-philosophical remarks on
the role of contrast in our lives,

> Through foul we follow fair,
> For had the world one face,
> And earth been bright as air,
> We had known neither place,
> (247, 8–11)

and with the example of the gods:

> The god that constant keeps
> Unto his deities
> Is poor in joys, and sleeps
> Imprison'd in the skies.
> This knew the wisest, who
> From Juno stole, below
> To love a bear or cow.
> (22–28)

The sly closing lines deify inconstancy. Not any intrinsic merit of
his current woman but variety as the spice of life is the subject of
this song, as well as of a better poem, "The Scrutiny." Instead of
answering an observer, the poet speaks directly to the lady, who
has just accused him of infidelity:

> Why should you swear I am forsworn,
> Since thine I vow'd to be?

> Lady, it is already morn,
>   And 'twas last night I swore to thee
> That fond impossibility.
>
> (251, 1–5)

The excuse is twofold: that so much time has already passed since
the previous night and that the oath was nugatory since it is logically impossible for one to swear to be another's. The first assertion, "Have I not lov'd thee much and long,/A tedious twelve
hours' space?" (6–7), is valid in the sense that emotional experience is its own measure of time—as is suggested by Dylan
Thomas' telling phrase, "a grief ago," or Donne's "For the first
twenty years since yesterday" or "His [=Love's] first minute after
noon, is night." But in this Lovelace poem the cynical speaker is
ironic.

Donning the mask of altruism, Lovelace advances another argument: "I must all other beauties wrong,/And rob thee of a new
embrace,/Could I still dote upon thy face" (8–10). There is nothing "in it" for him. He is leaving her in order to free her for new
erotic encounters and to give other women a chance at him. She
will give, as well as obtain, new pleasure by being freed of him:
"All joy in thy brown hair,/By others may be found" (11–12). His
choice of words—"lov'd thee . . . twelve hours," "rob thee . . .
of embrace," "dote upon thy face," and "joy in thy brown hair"
indicates the shallowness of his experience.

Then he reveals for the first time what his own actual benefits
would be—the pleasure of the variety of experience and the joy of
deflowering virgins: "But I must search the black and fair,/Like
skilful mineralists that sound/For treasure in unplough'd-up
ground" (13–15). In the last stanza he holds out hope for her:

> Then if, when I have lov'd my round,
>   Thou prov'st the pleasant she,
> With spoils of meaner beauties crown'd,
>   I laden will return to thee,
>   Ev'n sated with variety.
>
> (16–20)

If and when he finds the rest of womanhood uninteresting compared to her, he will take her back; she must submit to participa-

tion in a kind of beauty contest. His experience with the others will fulfill his male desire for varied sexual experience as well as make him newly aware how she is better than the "meaner" beauties. It will sate him, as he is now sated after a full night with her, and so at last make him a reliable, steady lover who will treasure her alone and for things other than sex. The man of full experience, "laden" and "crowned . . . with spoils," will be more attractive to her, a greater conquest. The important word, on which the poem ends, is "variety." His duty to himself and to the whole female sex is not to confine himself to one woman lest some other "she" be neglected for lack of scrutiny, investigation.

The persona—only half expecting to be believed and half believing himself—argues with the Donnean mixture of seriousness and archness; he laughs, even while speaking, at the ingenuity of his reasons. It is as though he were saying, "It is all over between us; we can part without sentiments and words, but since you women must have them, I'll give you what you want: Here are dozens of reasons and if some of them contradict each other, make of them what you will. They're ingenious reasons, though, you must admit, so that even though they have nothing to do with the way I actually feel and act, they might serve you as consolation. Play with them. Good bye." This scrutiny of their love exhibits, amid the medley of excuses, his cynicism; but in the last stanza he may well be deluding even himself into thinking that he actually would come back to her.

In an excellent analysis, Norman Holland reminds us that "scrutiny" then meant a critical or judicial inquiry. The first two stanzas are an inquiry into the rights and wrongs of jilting the lady; the last two, into the merits of jilting other women. The style of the poem reflects the paradox of just injustice, the "slick pretense of fairness," the tension between the conventional euphemisms ("beauties, embrace, joy") and the sordid aims. The poem moves away and comes back to the lady (even as the last stanza returns to the *ee* rhyme of the first), completing the paradox that to break his vow is reasonable.

The sexual symbolism in the third stanza is conscious, but its implications—comparing the finding of joy in a woman to discovering treasure in earth, dirt—are not. The imagery ("meaner beauties," "spoils") debases women and treats love as a possessing, a taking. The lover will not be possessed by the lady but will possess all others. The outer stanzas, conditional and argumentative, describe a man free to choose; but the word "must" in the middle stanzas suggests a compulsion, an insatiable drive. The poem is about detachment and involvement, about a man free from any one woman and captive to the idea of woman. It thus expresses Lovelace's major theme of imprisonment, of captivity and freedom.

Fearing to be engulfed by love, the lover must prove his separate existence by phallically degrading women, dispassionately "search[ing] black and fair" like "mineralists" probing dirt. "Scrutiny" comes from the Latin *scruta* (=garbage), and the lover is indeed picking over trash. He regards love as aggressive, debasing, directed at things; embraces can be robbed, "found," dug out of dirt. Holland rightly finds the close anticlimactic and ambiguous. The poet will not return as a developed personality but lapse back sensually sated, like an infant at its mother's bosom, and emotionally unsatisfied. Had the close been, Holland suggests, "Be thine, as thine I vow'd to be," it would suggest a rational, responsible choice instead of a childlike exhaustion.[1]

Another poem does not emphasize the importance of variety so much as it in one instance justifies inconstancy. The lover, again addressing the lady herself, insists as usual on the sincerity of his vows. Unusual is the kind of faithlessness he proceeds to accuse her of: "But once turn'd faithless to thyself, and old,/They then with thee incessantly grew cold" (262, 7–8). To have the lover excuse himself on the grounds that she broke the oath first is expectable but not that her faithlessness consisted of her growing old. Hardly consorting with what we consider gentlemanly behavior, it is based, like "You Are Deceived," on certain poems of execration by Horace. The concluding couplet summarizes the lover's position with a verve worthy of the personae of Donne or Suckling: "Then, changed thus, no more I'm bound to you,/Than swearing to a saint that proves untrue" (15–16).

II *How to Seduce a Woman*

The man's task in justifying promiscuity is easier if, besides emphasizing the importance to him of variety, he can persuade the woman of the benefits which will accrue to her. He will therefore reason that consummation of love is to be sought because a thing is not real until fulfilled, realized, used:

And we are taught that substance is,
If unenjoy'd, but th' shade of bliss.
                    (280, 43–44)

If still veiled from our sight,
What is't but eternal night?
. . . .
Not to be by man embrac'd
Makes that royal coin embas'd [=debased],
And this golden orchard waste.
. . . .
If it be not understood,
'Tis a diamond in mud.
. . . .
Thou art not bright, but to the eye.
                    (268, 3–4, 7–9, 18–21)

Moreover, woman is as fickle as man, because she too ultimately loves variety. The accusation of fickleness is at the heart of
"The Apostacy of One and but One Lady." The first half of each
stanza develops the idea of imperceptible change, while the second half treats of the woman's coldness. Then the poet attacks the
woman with bitter sarcasm:

Oh, she is constant as the wind
      That revels in an ev'ning's air!
Certain, as ways unto the blind,
      More real than her flatt'ries are;
Gentle, as chains that honour bind,
      More faithful than an Hebrew Jew,
But as the Devil not half so true.
                    (22–28)

The complimentary words—"constant," "certain," "gentle," "faithful"—introduce similes which highlight her fickleness by contrast.
The concluding, depreciatory, negative phrase, "But . . . not
half so," suggests a turn for the better which actually does not
take place—the final ironic comparison to the devil is the most
damning.
    The argument of woman's inconstancy not only is an excuse for
man's like behavior but also is related to the charge—conveniently

made when urging her to bed—that woman is as lustful as man, if
not more so. From time immemorial it has been supposed, in
Western civilization at least, that man, the sexual predator, is the
more erotic creature and that woman, the hunted one postponing
fulfillment as much as possible, accedes to his animal wishes not
because she enjoys the act but because she tries to please and
keep him. This assumption has been challenged by psychologists
only in recent years; but poets like Ovid, Donne, and Lovelace
occasionally suggested that woman derives much pleasure from
erotic encounters. In "Depose," the lady is urged to yield:

> So then enrich me with that treasure [which]
> Will but increase your store,
> And please me, fair one, with that pleasure [which]
> Must please you still the more.
> (249, 7–10)

The lover of "The Fair Beggar" declares, "There quench my heat,
and thou shalt sup/Worthy the lips that it must touch" (298, 19–
20); fulfilling his passion, she will receive something worthwhile
in return; for he but asks "the thing that thou dost crave" (4).

The use of the arguments of variety and universal concupis-
cence is only the opening gambit. To thrive, the lover must aban-
don the prostrate, tearful solicitations of courtly style. He must be
hard, demanding, and remorseless. If woman enjoys sex, why
should the man entreat her rather than she him? "Valiant Love"
deals extensively with the problem of the right approach for the
wooing man. Groans and tears will not do; "as if Love fir'd his
torch at a moist eye,/Or with his joys e'er crown'd the sad!" (294,
3–4). The lover must charge ahead:

> Oh let me live and shout, when I fall on!
> Let me ev'n triumph in the first attempt!
> Love's duellist from conquest's not exempt,
> When his fair murd'ress shall not gain one groan,
> And he expire ev'n in ovation.
> (5–9)

"Expire" is used in the common Elizabethan sense of "orgasm."
"Murd'ress" therefore signifies not the unrequiting haughty woman
but the one who brings about his "death." The point is that this

climax takes place "in ovation" or "triumph" because the lady is receptive to insistent, forceful advances, not to Petrarchan tears and groans. Military imagery, as old as Propertius, Ovid, and Horace, is utilized in the second stanza:

> No, I will vary storms with sun and wind;
>> Be rough, and offer calm condition,
>> March in, and pray 't, or starve the garrison.
> Let her make sallies hourly, yet I'll find,
> Though all beat off, she's to be undermin'd.
>> (14–18)

His talk is of direct and indirect methods; of storm and sunshine; of offers, sallies, roughness, marching in, undermining; of the give and take and the changing tactics in the chess game of love. "Henceforth none in tears dare love commence" (21) because such sentimentality is to give her the ascendancy, "Her thoughts i' th' full, his in th' eclipse"; "Since in your host that coward ne'er was fed,/Who to his prostrate e'er was prostrated" (26–27). The sexual overtones are aptly fused with the explicit military imagery: "On pain of having 's lance broke on her bed" (23).

Besides the lyrics which justify inconstancy or offer advice, Lovelace wrote outright seduction poems. In these brief addresses to a woman, the lover's intention to get her into bed as fast as possible is adorned with ingenious reasons in order to overcome her shyness, her religious and moral inhibitions, her suspicions. Though the roots of such poetry are to be found in Ovid, the major influence is again the early Donne. Lovelace's "Loose Saraband [1659]" is more of an invitation to drink than to erotic play, but the two activities are related. It opens with sexual overtones, "Nay, prithee dear, draw nigher,/Yet closer, nigher yet," and the succeeding lines celebrate the two kinds of pleasure jointly: "Here is a double fire,/A dry one and a wet/ . . . Mad love with wild canary" (324, 3–4, 8). There is an orderly succession of delights, for "wine makes all parts pliant" (44): "We drink our glass of roses,/ . . . Then, in our loyal chamber,/Refresh us with love's amber" (29, 31–2).

The persuasion is more sophistic and amusing in "Depose."

> Depose your finger of that ring,
> And crown mine with 't awhile.

> Now I restore 't—Pray does it bring
> 　Back with it more of soil?
> Or shines it not as innocent,
> As honest, as before 'twas lent?
> 　　　(249, 1–6)

One tactic of those who have to overcome another's adherence to a traditional moral concept is to indicate that the concept is amorphous because the word representing it is. Thus Marvell's lover speaks of "honor" as turning to dust, or Falstaff shows the word to be a mere breath; Edmund in *King Lear* does the like by repeating the words "base" and "legitimate" until they lose all meaning. In "Depose," the lover quibbles on "innocent" and "honest." He then applies the lesson to the lady, "so then enrich me with that treasure/Will but increase your store" (7–8). "Increase of store" refers to life experience as well as to sexual bliss. It can also mean pregnancy—though the woman is not meant to think of this last possibility: the lover winks past her shoulder at the reader.

The close of this charming piece of double entendre mingles appeals to the woman's equally intense desire for sexual play with appeals to her altruism to help one in distress in a way which cannot harm her at all:

> And please me, fair one, with that pleasure
> 　Must please you still the more:
> Not to save others is a curse
> The blackest, when y' are ne'er the worse.
> 　　　(9–12)

The last line thus leads back to the initial idea of the ring—a neat sexual symbol—left unsullied by its having been worn once on his finger.

"The Fair Beggar," a seduction poem of a special kind, is a late example of a series of Renaissance and Baroque exercises on a paradox: an attractive woman who would normally be herself the object of entreaties is forced to beg. Approached by her, the persona of the poem reverses his roles with her. His intentions are cryptic at first:

> Commanding asker, if it be
> 　Pity that you fain would have,

> Then I turn beggar unto thee,
>   And ask the thing that thou dost crave;
> I will suffice thy hungry need,
> So thou wilt but my fancy feed.
>   (297, 1–6)

Dwelling on the incongruity of a striking natural beauty covered with patched, dirty clothing, he adds,

> Yet happy he, that can but taste
>   This whiter skin, who thirsty is;
> Fools dote on satin motions [=marionets] lac'd,
>   The gods go naked in their bliss.
>   (13–16)

Ornate clothing would not do her any great good: "Cheap then are pearl embroideries,/That not adorn, but clouds thy waist" (25–26). He has something better in mind for her:

> Thou shalt be cloth'd above all price,
>   If thou wilt promise me embrac'd;
> We'll ransack neither chest or shelf,
> I'll cover thee with mine own self.
>   (27–30)

"Clothed" (27) sounds as if he is going to give her money and apparel which will enable her to dress in accord with her attractiveness, until "cover" (30) reveals what sort of dress he has in mind. Now the erotic invitation becomes more overt, with the sensual references to "heat," "sup," "lips," "breath":

> There quench my heat, and thou shalt sup
>   Worthy the lips that it must touch;
> Nectar from out the starry cup,
>   I beg thy breath not half so much.
>   (19–22)

This openness brings out the true meaning of earlier innocent-looking words like "thing," "crave," "fancy," "hungry," "need," "feed," "taste," "thirsty." And the sophistry, based on double entendre, grows apace too: "So both our wants suppli'd shall be,/

You'll give for love, I charity" (23–24). He ostensibly offers a simple quid pro quo arrangement: if she will yield, she will receive some alms. But a mischievous secondary meaning is that her wants as a sexually desiring woman will be fulfilled at the same time as his. "Charity" is perfect here: reminding us of the synonymous word "love," it refers to his "giving" something to a beggar and his kindness in satisfying her erotically.

The last line, "I starve your body, you my mind" (36), looks back to "hungry . . . feed" (5–6): his not giving her any money is merely to deprive her body of food, whereas her unwillingness to yield is to starve his mind, his fancy. He has turned the projected sexual intercourse into something spiritual; because it satisfies her too, it is an act of charity, of giving, on both sides. Her rejecting such a spiritual matter is therefore harsher than his mere refusal to give her filthy lucre.

This amusing, well-constructed poem succeeds because of the byplay throughout between the lover's erotic demands and his ostensible response to her request for charity. He nicely confounds the male's active role in sexual encounters with the giving of something to the beggar-lady. Image patterns are carefully woven into the texture of the lyric: the theme of hunger and supping, like that of clothing and covering, is used consistently in a literal and figurative erotic sense.

Both themes arise from the lady's beggarly condition. The main signs of poverty—hunger and poor apparel—are naturally turned into sexual analogues: the hunger of the flesh; the sipping and feeding in sex play; the necessary undressing which renders the actual condition of her clothing irrelevant and turns his body into sufficient cover for her. He begins by suggesting that her clothing is unbecoming to her beautiful body but what sounds like a compliment is transformed into a request, growing logically out of his prior remarks, that she remove the clothes. Thus in the very act of praising and flattering her, he makes veiled advances to her. And through the poem runs the paradox of the man who, normally in a beseeching position vis-à-vis a beautiful woman, now finds the situation reversed. She asks for something gratuitous, and he returns the request to her. She asks for literal food and clothes, and he, exploiting his opportunity, offers her figurative food and covering.

M. J. O'Regan has recently discovered what may be the ultimate source of this motif, a poem by the Spanish cleric and

satirist Quevedo. Studying the metamorphoses of the popular
theme in Achillini, Tristan, Malleville, Ayres (twice), and Lovelace, O'Regan traces the decline, as he sees it, of a Baroque theme.
In its earliest version, a lady greedy for rich gifts is told she possesses a figurative treasure in her beauty. Subsequent versions, in
order to heighten the antithesis, present the lady as poor in fact;
but a certain balance, sensuousness, and esthetic beauty in Quevedo's version is lost. The conceit is, moreover, reshaped by the
nature of the culture as much as by the character of the poet who
uses it. Thus Lovelace's poem, sophistic, sensual, cynical in the
libertine, bluff English manner of Donne and Suckling, is far from
the gallantries of the Spanish and Italian, or from the *précieux*
abstractions and curtsies of the French. His ego at all times present, Lovelace's persona indulges in bargaining rather than in
eulogy. The style is colloquial, not oratorical; homely images re-
place the lush jewel imagery with which the genre began in Quevedo's poem.[2] For all of its indebtedness to earlier poems and to
the Donne style, Lovelace's "Fair Beggar" is one of his best lyrics.
It may not be "original" in our sense of the word—few of his
poems are—but its logic, imagery, and wit are strikingly ordered,
as in Donne and Marvell at their best. Its sophistry is amusing,
thorough, persuasive. Its individual lines and stanzas have vigor.
It is a gem of adaptation and composition.

III   *The Moment of Bliss and the Age of Gold*

Lovelace wrote few passages depicting the sexual congress, for
here again, his master, Donne, showed the way. It has often been
noted that despite the libertinism, the invitations to dalliance, the
talk of inconstancy in Donne's early poetry, there is little explicit
sexuality. Except for Elegy XVIII and XIX, Donne's poems have
an austerity that is the more striking when compared with the
directness of Suckling and Carew. His poems are *about* the sexual
encounter; they dramatize the steps leading to it and the means
by which the lovers extricate themselves from it; they do not describe it. The same characteristic holds true of Lovelace. He occasionally uses suggestive phrases, to be sure: "undermining,"
"treasure in unploughed-up ground," "lance broken on her bed";
or, after speaking innocently of the muff in which the lady's fingers are wrapped, he concludes abruptly that, while lay lovers
would be happy just to see that piece of attire he rates "not this

outward bliss enough,/But still contemplate must the hidden
muff" (316, 24–25). "In Allusion . . ." begins innocently enough
with good old Petrarchan gentility, "How often have my tears/In-
vaded your soft ears" (313, 3–4); but it suddenly veers into male
candor:

> Know then, I would melt
> On every limb I felt,
> And on each naked part
> Spread my expanded heart,
> That not a vein of thee
> But should be fill'd with me;
> Whilst on thine own down I
> Would tumble, pant, and die.
> (33–40)

The refrain, "Then understand you not, fair choice,/This language
without tongue or voice?" (1–2), now turns out to be applicable
to erotic gestures. The lover has become frank because she did not
understand the full import of his words. The implication is that
the courtly Petrarchan wooer is not really so different in his ultimate aims from the out-and-out seducer.

The abrupt shift from genteel sentiments to scabrous notions
recurs in "To Amarantha, That She would Dishevel her Hair."
After discreetly urging the lady in the first four stanzas to unbind
her hair and let it flow freely in the wind, the poet changes his
tune:

> See, 'tis broke! Within this grove,
> The bower and the walks of love,
>   Weary lie we down and rest,
>   And fan each other's panting breast.
>
> Here we'll strip and cool our fire
> In cream below, in milk-baths higher.
> (248, 17–22)

The last line contains sexuality feebly dressed in "metaphysical
wit." [3]

The most explicit, detailed, and esthetically satisfying of Lovelace's erotic poems is the rhapsodic fantasy, "Love Made in the

First Age." Cast in the form of an invitation to dalliance, it turns
into a revery of free love and innocent sexuality, a nostalgic dream
of Arcady. It begins with a contrast between antiquity and the
current age; in olden days, words were expressive of essence or
were not used. There follows a vision of "yea-saying": "When
cursed No stain'd no maid's bliss,/And all discourse was summ'd
in Yes,/And naught forbade, but to forbid" (328, 10–12). The poetry grows lush with description: "Love, then unstinted, love did
sip,/And cherries pluck'd fresh from the lip,/On cheeks and roses
free he fed" (13–15). Shakespeare's "golden lads and lasses" are
shown in a new light: "Lasses like Autumn plums did drop,/And
lads indifferently did crop/A flower and a maidenhead" (16–18).
The casualness of their actions is nicely conveyed by the *zeugma*
(two or more words governed in different ways by another, for
the sake of incongruity) here and in the next stanza, where the
imagery of drinking and eating, as prominent as in the "Fair Beggar," mingles with parts of the female anatomy:

> Then unconfined each did tipple
> Wine from the bunch, milk from the nipple,
>   Paps tractable as udders were;
> Then equally the wholesome jellies
> Were squeez'd from olive-trees and bellies,
>   Nor suits of trespass did they fear.
>   (19–24)

Lovelace is so carried away by his dream world that he attrib-
utes to it contradictory traits. Having spoken of the easy way in
which the young disposed of maidenheads, he abruptly paints a
tender picture of constancy:

> Both broken faith and th' cause of it,
> All-damning gold, was damn'd to th' Pit;
>   Their troth, seal'd with a clasp and kiss,
> Lasted until that extreme day
> In which they smil'd their souls away,
>   And in each other breath'd new bliss.
>   (31–36)

Seeing a world, our world, in which some women are inhibited
from yielding to the men they like and in which others are unin-

hibited but also inconstant, he evokes an ideal world where the contrary of both will obtain—women who are generous with their bodies yet constant at the same time. Or, more likely, the inconsistency derives from an imperfect fusion of different versions of the golden age—the libertine world painted by Tasso and, on the other hand, the moral golden age described by Guarini in his implicit retort to Tasso, a world where each woman is faithful to one man, where "husband" and "lover" is the same.

Petrarchan tears and groans are banished, nor has the Fall and consequent sense of sin taken place:

> Because no fault, there was no tear;
> No groan did grate the granting ear;
>   No false foul breath their del'cat smell:
> No serpent kiss poison'd the taste,
> Each touch was naturally chaste,
>   And their mere sense a miracle.
>   (37–42)

The accoutrements of our world—clothing, ornaments, tables, beds—are unnecessary. "Naked as their own innocence/ . . . They went" (43, 45).

Like "The Grasshopper," this poem bristles with venerable themes and conventions. The Greeks and Romans believed in a golden age from which the world had degenerated: Horace, in Epode ii, depicts it as a life of hard but rewarding work; Virgil, in Eclogue iv, as an idyl amid natural fertility. Virgil's golden age, though leisurely and pleasurable, is morally decorous; it is evoked by later Christian writers like Boethius and Chaucer. In contrast to it, the love elegists preferred recalling the special erotic advantages and joys of times gone by. Tibullus (I, iii; II, iii) speaks of "troops of young men [who] meet in sport with gentle maidens, and love never lets his warfare cease"; Ovid (I, x) and Propertius (IV, xiii) dream of days before money and shame ruled—"it was no sin to see goddesses naked." This outlook was somehow revived in the late Middle Ages when Jean de Meun's continuation of the *Romance of the Rose* juxtaposed a lax golden age with arguments depicting Goddess Nature not as the revelation of universal reason but as the instinctive life.

Louis Bredvold has shown how such erotic poetry reflected a

HUNT LIBRARY
CARNEGIE-MELLON UNIVERSITY

philosophic onslaught on "Natural Law." The Stoics, and, later, Cicero and the Christians, taught that a universal, immutable law of nature was the basis of the moral code and had prevailed in the golden age when men held all in common. The Epicureans and Skeptics, denying the existence of such a law, pictured the golden age as morally unrestrained. The Renaissance's infatuation with antiquity brought about a revival of these pagan, skeptical ideas. Rabelais's Abbey of Theleme, with its motto, "Do what you want" (cf. Lovelace's "nought forbade, but to forbid"), harks back to such a lax golden age. Tasso goes further in his famous "O bèlla età de l'òro" chorus in *Aminta*. He evokes a time when honor, bred of custom and opinion, did not yet tyrannize over lovers' hearts and veil virgins' breasts; a time when all followed the laws of nature in a life of nudity, sexual freedom, and "golden hairs . . . spread unto the wind," for the rule was "s'ei piace, ei lice [if it pleases, it's permitted]." The direct attack on "honor" becomes the distinctive characteristic of Renaissance reveries of the golden age.

The man who most developed the philosophical ramifications was Montaigne. Arriving at a skeptical position which ruled out belief in universal moral truth, he turned from trust in either a Law of Nature or custom and convention to a philosophy of individualism based on Nature—Nature as the instinctual desires of each individual and uncorrupted by man's customs and laws. In his "Cannibals" essay, Montaigne warmly responded to the relatively uncorrupted primitive life; and this philosophical "libertinism" formed an important current in late Renaissance thought. In England, Donne, like Shakespeare and others, read Montaigne carefully. Donne's early erotic poems, notably "Communitie," "Confined Love," and Elegy III and XVII, appeal continually to Nature for justification of sensuality—for setting man the example of liberty, change, freedom from society's restraints. Love is classed with the other appetites as a purely physical reaction; and man is, with the beasts, a creature of nature only. Inconstancy is a good thing. The laws of society, though pretending to absolute validity, are the result of custom; and their supposed sacredness is but "opinion."

These ideas developed concurrently in England and France, with French influences at the same time making themselves felt in England. In France, Montaigne's ideas were turned to poetic use by such as St. Amant and Théophile de Viau, who was banished for two years for remarks like "J'approuve qu'un chacun suive en tout la nature./Son empire est plaisant, et sa loy n'est pas dure [Let everyone in everything follow Nature,/Whose sway is pleasant, and law not hard]." They wrote a poetry of *jouissance*(enjoyment), which at its best dramatized Montaigne's ideas, presenting in a garden of unfallen innocence the libertine exaltation of sexuality and the abolition of honor and female chastity. The importation of French ideas into England was helped, ironically, by the advent of Charles I's French wife. Her own taste was for the diluted fashionable *précieux* platonism, but the English poets, already writing in the early Donne manner, gravitated to what interested them. Thomas Stanley translated St. Amant's "Jouissance" and Théophile's poems. Fairfax, Fane, Cotton, and others made similar adaptation; Suckling traveled in France, translated miscellaneous lyrics, and was the most responsive to this current.

Whether coming from Italy or France, such philosophic and literary currents stimulated a genre of poems which contained either a garden of love or a vision of the golden age; invited the young lady to dalliance; argued in libertine fashion for naked Nature and against the tyrants Honor and Custom; described in rich detail the results of such logic, sexual joys; and insisted on the innocence of it all, often by comparing man to the amoral plants and animals.

Under Elizabeth, Daniel had translated Tasso's golden age chorus; and Fairfax, the Italian's *Jerusalem Delivered*. In that epic, Armida's erotic bower of bliss and her song inviting to dalliance are the bases of Acrasia's bower of bliss in Spenser's *Faerie Queene*. These works, however, hedge by presenting the libertine ideas as objectionable; in Daniel's "Ulysses and the Siren," Milton's "Comus," as in Tasso's and Spenser's narratives, Satanic figures express them. But in the seventeenth century, when the genre is full-blown, no such qualifications exist. The ideas appear without, as it were, quotation marks and as values shared by poet and reader. Carew's "Rapture"—one of the earliest, most famous, and best of these—had a clear influence on an imposing list of works: Thomas Randolph's "A Pastorall Courtship," "Upon Love fondly refus'd for Conscience sake," "In . . . Georgii Goringe"; Suckling's "His Dream"; Herrick's modest "Apparition . . . Elizium"; William Cartwright's "A Song of Dalliance," "Beauty and Deniall";

Cleveland's "To Chloris: A Rapture"; Stanley's "Love's Innocence"; Katherine Philips' mild "Country Life"; Mrs. Aphra Behn's
"Golden Age," "Voyage to the Isle of Love," "The Prospect and
the Bower of Bliss"; and numerous brief lyrics. Out of this milieu
sprang Lovelace's "Love Made in the First Age."[4]

Such poems are in one respect an outgrowth of the situation
common in genteel courtly poetry. They present a change in the
Petrarchan lover's attitude and psychology. If his appeals continue to be in vain, he begins to place the blame for the lady's
coldness not on his own insufficiency but on false notions of honor
spread by Christianity. He then conjures up a world free of these
notions; he tries to remake a world he never made. He appeals to
a different life style, to the enjoyment of unconfined sexuality, acceptance of life's pleasure through the body, and rejection of all
laws, mores, conventions, restraints. He must convince the lady
not only of the joys in store for her, but also of the larger philosophic sanctions for her yielding. He undermines the traditional
morality and suggests how an earlier, different moral arrangement
has been just as feasible. To arouse her, he sketches a way of life
they can join by acting in accord with its dictates and mores, a life
which justifies their dissenting from a morality now seen as merely
the custom of a time and place. We are a long way from the reverent worship of "honor" usually ascribed to Lovelace.

Such a lyric expresses the secular Lovelace's nostalgia for a life
free of Christian austerity. The critique never takes the form of a
direct attack on Christianity itself—that is rare in England before
Blake and Burns—but dotes on a world innocent of the new dispensation, on what might have been without it. The golden age
never existed but is a vivid projection of an ideal of life. Renaissance art indulged in such pagan reveries in paintings like Gio-
vanni Bellini's "Feast of the Gods," Luca Signorelli's "Pan," Pietro
di Cosimo's pictorial ruminations on primitivism.[5]

"Love Made in the First Age" is not a perfect poem. Like many
other only partly successful Lovelace pieces—"La Bella Bona
Roba," "Cupid Far Gone," "A Black Patch"—it is static; it iterates
a good idea in a sequence of images instead of developing it.
Some of its images are in fact, as Geoffrey Walton describes them,
exaggerated and humorless or, in Rufus Blanshard's word, grotesque. Donne's erotic elegies have a logical coherence, a dynamic
forward movement, a daring wittiness and consistency in imagery,

while Carew's "Rapture" has a sensuality, a persuasiveness, a real pagan feeling that leave Lovelace's poem behind. But the Lovelace poem is confronted with tough competitors. It remains a good poem, perhaps even one of Lovelace's better ones. And individual lines and images in it are very good indeed.

CHAPTER 7

Imagery

I *Traditional*

THE study of the use, separately and as part of recurring patterns, of images in a poem, play, or novel is a recent phenomenon. This approach has, despite inevitable excesses, renewed our response to the standard works of literature by making us aware of the many complex ways in which genius coerces the reader into accepting its vision of life. Image patterns—when combined with each other and when working in concert with rhetoric, character portrayal, moral insight, and dramatic development—subtly heighten our appreciation of the work of art. While not changing the direction or explicit meaning of the work, these verbal spotlights affect the overtones and nuances. They are a kind of unobtrusive, persuasive underlining. Not advanced in accordance with the laws of logic, the ideas and feelings they arouse cannot be refuted. Thus, in several of Lovelace's poems, everything seems relevant and cooperative: the balance of references to the vocations of love and chivalry in "Wars"; begging, thirst, clothing in "The Fair Beggar"; the ring in "Depose."

The bulk of Lovelace's imagery consists of conventional Petrarchan matter. The beloved, or her eye, is like the sun; the lover, burning and freezing, woos with sighs and tears; his heart is literally toyed with by the lady. Little allegories about the heart were also closely related to those of Cupid, the mythological personification of love. The heart's running afoul of Cupid is the subject of "A Loose Saraband [1649]." This poem is but one of a number of anecdotes about the naked god of love which are part of a venerable tradition running through the Latin elegists, the *Anacreontea*, the *Greek Anthology*. Cupid's adventures form a set of brief allegories of the amatory experience. In the seventeenth century, Jonson, Herrick, Cowley, and even Milton adapted such poems.

Since Cupid is responsible for the emotional travail of the lover, a state of war exists between them. This conflict is the subject of

"The Duel." While the lover's attention was directed elsewhere, Cupid assaulted his senses. Trying to bring the god to account, the lover finds he must resort to trial by combat; and the duel takes place on the grounds of Venus. The lover disrobes because that is the proper mode for love and because Cupid himself is naked. But in combat he finds his enemy to be evanescent: "When my arm to its true distance came,/I nothing touch'd but a fantastic flame" (333, 23–24). The concluding stanza provides a moral tag to the anecdote, asserting that the god—the emotional experience he represents—is a mere will-o'-the-wisp, to be overcome easily if we but realized his insubstantiality: "This, this is Love we daily quarrel so,/And idle Don-Quixotery:/ . . ./The only way t' undo this enemy/Is to laugh at the boy, and he will cry" (25–26, 29–30).

At other times, love can seem more menacing: the elusive, mischievous little god runs amuck in "Cupid Far Gone." The results, though somewhat comical, are attempts at, among other dastardly acts, incest, pederasty, seduction of the gods:

> See! at's own mother he is offering,
> His finger now fits any ring:
> Old Cybele he would enjoy,
> And now the girl, and now the boy.
> He proffers Jove a back caress,
> And all his love in the Antipodes.
> (333, 7–12)

Appearing like the typical, worldly Donnean seducer, "Now like a fury he belies/Myriads of pure virginities;/And swears, with this false frenzy hurl'd,/There's not a virtuous she in all the world" (21–24). He ranges into hell and upsets everything there too. Relating Cupid's madness without giving cause or conclusion, the poem dramatizes, with a tableau of the god of love become his own victim, the irrationality and power of that passion.

Sometimes victimization has the reverse effect—greater maturity. In "Love Enthroned," Cupid falls in love with Lucasta and mends his ways: "He doth his glorious darts dispense, . . . /Love Justice is become,/And doth the cruel doom" (315, 10, 13–14). The old pains of unrequited love are gone; he makes lovers accord. The whole world, even virgins and nature, responds to him.

The result is a love idyll, a golden age as in "Love Made in the First Age":

> Whilst to his altars now
>   The frozen Vestals bow,
> And strict Diana, too, doth go
> A-hunting with his fear'd, exchanged bow.
>
> Th' embracing seas and ambient air
>   Now in his holy fires burn;
> Fish couple, birds and beasts in pair
>   Do their own sacrifices turn.
>   (21–28)

Cupid is also overcome in "Love Conquer'd." At the beginning he, in a cynical and coldhearted mood, is envious of mutual love. Shooting his arrows at the lady's "constant marble heart" in order to set up discord, he finds to his surprise that they boomerang and infect him. A reversal takes place as he becomes victim of the very unrequited love he had tried to propagate:

> Now the prince of fires burns!
>   Flames in the lustre of her eyes;
> Triumphant she refuses, scorns;
> He submits, adores, and mourns,
>   And is his vot'ress' sacrifice.
>   (255, 11–15)

Subjected thus, he recants and sets the constant lovers up as models for a new dispensation. He has learned through sympathetic identification.

A dethronement of Cupid occurs in the epithalamium, "The Triumphs." Part of the usual wedding procession includes the god of love, but this wedding is a Christian one. A naked, sexless "youth of more than godlike form" (346, 83)—Heavenly Love— walks beside the mischievous god he has displaced and disarmed:

> By his [Heavenly Love's] bright hand,
> A boy of worse than earthly stuff did stand,
>   His bow broke, his fires out, and his wings clipp'd,

> And the black slave from all his false flames stripp'd;
> Whose eyes were new restor'd but to confess
> This day's bright bliss and his own wretchedness.
> (346, 87–92)

This tableau dramatizes the end of the uncertain, mutable, worldly love between men and women, and the beginning of the wedded couple's eternal love sanctified in heaven. The contrast between the two Cupids no doubt owes something to such works as the Neo-Platonic hymns to Love and Heavenly Love by Spenser.

Despite duelling with the little god or wishing to overthrow his powers, the poet regards him with ambivalence. Cupid was traditionally compared to, or described in terms of, a fly or bee: "This, this is Love we daily quarrel so,/ . . . We wound the air for a fly" (333, 25, 27–28). In some poems Cupid, in others the bee or fly, is attracted to the beloved. Herrick pointed out the obvious parallel and the reason for the ambivalence: "Thus, like a Bee, Love-gentle still doth bring/Hony to salve, where before did sting." The similarity is enhanced by their rivalry: "His fatal enemy the bee . . . /Ne'er half so nettled him as he is now" (333, 3, 6).

Another rich source of imagery was Classical mythology. Lovelace makes predictable references to Venus, Apollo, the Graces, Atlas, Juno, Proteus, Ceres, Bacchus, Neptune, Diana. This "Classical drapery," part of the vocabulary of all educated persons in the Renaissance, was one way of giving dignity to verses. On the other hand, the only Christian image pattern is of angels. Although beings who traverse and see our world but are above its tensions and emotions, they paradoxically feel more deeply for us. Their disembodied, high-soaring, free nature is their salient characteristic; and man at his best reaches such a state: the separated lovers meet "Above the highest sphere . . . /Unseen, unknown, and greet as angels greet" (246, 17–18); the resolute, emotionally fulfilled Cavalier knows in jail such liberty as "Angels alone, that soar above/Enjoy" (285, 31–32).

II *Scientific Lore and Paradox*

One of the hallmarks of Donne's style is the use, even in erotic poetry, of references to Scholastic philosophy and to the latest scientific developments. This characteristic sprang from his great curiosity and omnivorous reading. Lacking either his erudition or probing mind, Lovelace could not match the master's ease in alien disciplines. His passing references of this sort do not make the meaning clearer or more powerful. They merely decorate, as in the use of semi-technical words, "anatomy," "epitome," or the more technical *aurum fulminans*. Thus, a curious belief in the field of meteorology was that shooting stars turned to jelly; in speaking of a beautiful lady grown old, Lovelace's persona swears, "By the glorious light/Of both those stars, of which, their spheres bereft,/Only the jelly's left" (262, 12–14). Or he refers to newer, more "scientific" matter: "Since now wisest know/(And this to Galileo's judgment owe)/The palsy earth itself is every jot/As frail, inconstant, waving" (348, 19–22). The earth's movements become a metaphor for the flux in human life.

Beyond these concrete references, there runs through Lovelace's poems a quasi-philosophic sense of the contradiction of things. Facts of the human condition are that we appreciate an object only by reference to its possible absence; that value is relative and circumstantial; that good may grow out of evil. This principle of contrast is at work in even the most trivial events. The beautiful singing of a nurse, for instance, more than compensates for the irritation caused by the children's crying: "Thus have I heard to children's cries/The fair nurse 'stil such lullabies/That well all said, for what there lay,/The pleasure did the sorrow pay" (293, 19–22).

Such facts are paradoxes, and with them the poet makes us see reality afresh, makes us aware of the difference between what we thought and what we now know. We have seen the operation of paradox in the famous poems on being in prison, on separating from the beloved, or on drinking intoxicating beverages. The whole spectrum of amatory experience is, of course, deeply involved with paradox. The Petrarchan lover dwells on the oscillation between extremes, the concurrent experience of opposites, on what, in short, Lovelace calls "All lovers' pleasing wretchedness" (277, 14). Such paradoxes are the expression of the "odi et amo" in every love. In the poems of seduction, a different sort of paradox prevails, as the lover deliberately confounds physical and spiritual entities in order to justify illicit sexual intercourse. He chooses "variety," moreover, because man is best aware of the existence of some entity or quality through acquaintance with its opposite or with something different in some way: "Indians smell not their nest;/A Swiss or Finn tastes best/The Spices of the East" (247, 12–14). Yet contrast is a two-edged sword: Love may create happiness: "After th' eclipse our sun doth brighter shine" (357, 6); or unhappiness: "And deal a larger measure in our pain,/By showing joy, then hiding it again" (261, 23–24).

In "To Chloe" the lover finds that his own passion is heightened by his awareness of his friend's equally intense attraction to her:

> Its use and rate values the gem,
> Pearls in their shells have no esteem;
> And I being sun within thy sphere,
> 'Tis my chief beauty thinner lights shine there.
> (249, 13–16)

The presence of the rival may well be the cause of the love; we are such social creatures that our emotions are conditioned from without:

> The us'rer heaps unto his store
> By seeing others praise it more;
> Who not for gain or want doth covet,
> But 'cause another loves doth love it.
> (17–20)

This dialectic is brought out in a different way in the poems dramatizing duels between various creatures.

Paradoxes appear as well in poems having to do with matters other than love, imprisonment or the strange ways of little beasts. Books which systematize fencing or chess bring us to the mystery of vicarious experience: "Be able to dispute i' th' field,/And combat in the schools" (278, 1–2, 11–12). Paradoxes are prominent no less in moral considerations, Stoic or Christian. The poem on Lely's painting of Charles I contains phrases like "grief triumphant," "happy misery," "victorious sorrow." The elegy on Cassandra Cotton proclaims the essential Christian paradox of existence: "You are more dead and buried than she" (291, 57–60). The elegy on Princess Katherine, "Born, Christened, Buried in One Day," begins with well-controlled Christian antitheses, which are maintained, with much ingenuity, to the end.

III *Quotidian*

There remain several groups of images—eye, silence, mirror, dreams, hair, clothing—which are prosaic matters of everyday life and are related to the love life in interesting ways. Perhaps in exploiting such homely detail, as in his poems on small creatures, lay Lovelace's talent, which he unfortunately did not develop sufficiently. Of these images, that of the eye is variously used. It may be an index of states of mind or moral significances, the site from which character shines forth, the source of tears and expressions of grief, the mirror in which the lover sees himself reflected, the means by which love is generated, or a lethal instrument. Not only the lady but also the toad and the spider, in their mortal combat, use killing looks: "Met the two dreaded enemies,/Having their weapons in their eyes" (339, 7–8). In the ensuing battle the spider triumphs by destroying the toad's eyes, even as the reader of a book on fencing or chess can "win with a look" (278, 6; 358, 4).

Though for most of us only an instrument of sight, the eye may also be a means of *in*sight, spiritual vision: "Oh stay that covetous hand; first turn all eye,/All depth and mind; then mystically spy/Her soul's fair picture, her fair soul's" (289, 1–3). The paradoxical nature of sight and insight has been embodied in the careers of Oedipus, Tiresias, and of Gloucester in *King Lear*; to these Lovelace adds Galileo, who, though later blind, was an "oculist" by dint of studying the eye of heaven: "The blind and late heaven's eye's great oculist" (357, 2). If one must "turn all eye" for insight, a different transformation is associated with intense esthetic experience: "Sing, Laura, sing whilst silent are the spheres,/And all the eyes of heaven are turn'd to ears" (338, 1–2); or, expressed in another way,

> But as, at Mecca's tomb, the devout blind
> Pilgrim, great husband of his sight and mind,
> Pays to no other object this chaste price,
> Then with hot earth anoints out both his eyes:
> So, having seen your dazzling glories' store,
> Is it enough, and sin for to see more?
>   (344, 13–18)

We associate important events with sounds, often loud ones; but the potent eyes function in silence. In Lovelace's "Orpheus to Beasts," the poet-musician, lamenting the death of his wife, subordinates his kind of harmony to hers:

> Oh, could you view the melody
>   Of ev'ry grace,
> And music of her face,
>   You'd drop a tear.
> Seeing more harmony
>   In her bright eye,
> Than now you hear.
>   (258, 8–14)

The words "view," "seeing," "eye" help convey the point that beauty, though expressed here musically ("melody," "music," "harmony"), is apprehended by the eye instead of the ear, in the sense that Goethe called architecture "frozen music": beauty of character, like physical attractiveness, is a silent music. Thus Lovelace insists, after ridiculing his own inability to sing, on the beautiful sounds within himself:

> Yet can I music too; but such
> As is beyond all voice or touch;
> My soul so full of harmony,
> My mind can in fair order chime,
> My loudest music is within.
>   (294, 53–57)

Silence paradoxically is a greater form of communication than words:

> So then this silence doth reveal
> No thought of negligence, but zeal;
> For, as in adoration,
> This is love's true devotion:
>   Children and fools the words repeat,
>   But anch'rites pray in tears and sweat.
>   (262, 13–18)

Lovers sooner or later enter the phase in which operates "this language without tongue or voice" (313, 2). Not only the "silent chimes" of tears, but

> The rheto'ric of my hand
> Woo'd you to understand;
> Nay, in our silent walk
> My very feet would talk,
> My knees were eloquent,
> And spake the love I meant.
> (314, 23–28)

> And now they gaze, and sigh, and weep,
> Whilst each cheek doth the other's steep,
> Whilst tongues as exorcis'd are calm;
> Only the rhet'ric of the palm
> Prevailing pleads, until at last,
> They chain'd in one another fast.
> (310, 319–24)

In reflecting the objects it sees, the eye is sometimes compared to the mirror. In "Lucasta's Fan," the lover notes that the sun retires in shame before the lady's superior face reflected in the "crystal mirror" fixed upon the fan. The efficacy of the mirror prompts in Lucasta a self-adulation reminiscent of Belinda's rites of pride in the Pope's "Rape of the Lock." Against this expressed desire for self-containment, withdrawal and secretiveness, Lovelace's unrequited lover exclaims bitterly to the gods:

> "Ah, show their empty strength!" The gods accord.
> Now fall'n the brittle favourite lies, and burst.
> Amaz'd Lucasta weeps, repents, and flies
> To her Alexis, vows herself accurs'd
> If hence she dress herself but in his eyes.
> (267, 32–36)

This little anecdote, a rendering of the Narcissus myth, sketches the dangers to the haughty lady of becoming so rapt in her own attractiveness—a temptation common to the sex—as to yield to sterile, solitary idolatry instead of warm human contact. The mirror functions as a changing symbol. A mechanical device which reproduces reality and by which to dress oneself, it has the power to present an objective image of the self and so be the object of one's attention, the focus of one's emotions. It becomes the icon of self-love, a visible token of a spiritual imbalance. A contrast is set up between the haughty Petrarchan lady whose interest is centered on a cold piece of glass bearing an image of herself and the yielding woman who, if she must see herself, can best do so in the warm living eyes of her beloved.

The idea of a woman whose essence is reducible to her mirror and feather recurs in "Advice," "The toy that we, too true, a mistress call,/Whose looking-glass and feather weighs up all" (349, 33–34). The emptiness or unreality of the mirror's image suggests that the person worshiping it is as superficial as it: "Court her as her adorers do their glass,/Though that as much of a true substance has" (362, 69–70). The insubstantiality of the mirror image is remarked as well in "The Apostacy": in the midst of ironical lines on woman's constancy, the lover says,

> This woman's love no time can rase [=erase],
> Hard'ned like ice in the sun's eye,
> Or your reflection in a glass,
> Which keeps possession though you pass.
> (295, 11–14)

The mirror is, of course, unable to keep an image once the source of it has left; what then remains in the mirror? The ultimate mystery is intimated by the image, in the midst of a description of calm sea and sky, of mirror confronting mirror: "Whilst th' air puts on its sleekest, smoothest face,/And each doth turn the other's looking-glass" (355, 21–22).

In the light of the mirror's metaphysical emptiness, a substitute is presented in the pastoral. Aramantha, living the life *à la rustica*, has no need of elaborate cosmetics or gaudy mirrors to keep her beautiful; the surface of the pail of water in which she washes provides her with all the self-regard that is necessary: "Her pail's all this, in which wet glass/She both doth cleanse and view her face" (303, 25–26). A higher kind of mirror is pointed to by the song, "Strive Not"; the lover should dress himself "in her fair soul's immac'late glass" and "by reflection" see a "true fineness" (313, 10), even as the haughty woman must learn to see herself in the lover's eye.

Where the mirror mechanically reflects reality, however fleetingly or imperfectly, the dream is an interior, organic process of duplicating, reshaping, and modifying reality. It is a mirror of the mind, a mirror which reflects also the invisible movements of feelings, memories, sensations.

Some dreams present a life more pleasant. Such "dreams" may be literal or figurative. In urging his brother Francis not to undertake a sea trip, Lovelace depicts graphically the dangers of the sea, to which one may suddenly awaken from happy dreams:

> Dream, dream still,
> Lull'd in Dione's cradle, dream, until
> Horror awake your sense, and you now find
> Yourself a bubbled pastime for the wind.
> (348, 11–14)

The joy of having been with a friend is comparable to various dreams:

> Thus, after view of all the Indies' store,
> The slave returns unto his chain and ear;
> Thus poets, who all night in blest heav'ns dwell,
> Are call'd next morn to their true living hell;
> So I unthrifty . . . 'cause wanting you,
> And what substantial riches I possess
> I must to these unvalu'd dreams confess.
> (347, 140–44, 145–47)

The awakening disrupts the happy, transient dream and returns one to one's pains. It is then a matter of temperament or mood whether one, like the poet here, is grateful for the relief provided by the dream or, like Dante's Francesca, feels the present pain the more as a result of contrast:

> Vain dreams of love! that only so much bliss
> Allow us, as to know our wretchedness;
> And deal a larger measure in our pain,
> By showing joy, then hiding it again.
> (261, 21–24)

Lovers facing separation turn to dreams as an experience in which reunion is possible; Alexis describes parting in terms of a sleep in which souls are exchanged. The dream can be so pleasant that it may be preferred to the reality: "And oh! if night us undivided make,/Let us sleep still, and sleeping, never wake!" (261, 31–32). Thus, the speaker of "Love Made in the First Age," having described to the obdurate Chloris a world sexually free, dismisses her in favor of a sort of psychic masturbation: "Whilst, ravish'd with these noble dreams,/And crowned with mine own soft beams,/Enjoying of myself I lie" (329, 58–60). In spite of sharp contrasts, however, we sometimes cannot tell which is dream and which reality:

> Now, as a prisoner new cast,
> Who sleeps in chains that night his last,
> Next morn is wak'd with a reprieve,
> And from his trance not dream bid live,
> Wonders (his sense not having scope)
> Who speaks, his friend or his false hope.
> (307, 197–202)

More intimately connected with Lovelace's erotic poetry is the imagery of hair and clothing. The beloved's hair, a common subject in all love lyrics, is at the heart of "Song to Amarantha, That She would Dishevel her Hair": "Amarantha sweet and fair,/Ah braid no more that shining hair!/As my curious hand or eye,/Hovering round thee let it fly" (247, 1–4). To C. V. Wedgwood, this casual request is a sign of the gradual displacement in England of the older Italian and Spanish influences by the French. The Elizabethans liked their women's hair stiff and rigidly pattered, as can be gauged from portraits and from references, like Donne's, to the mistress's "coronet of wire"; the newer fashion was for flowing ringlets. Lovelace proceeds to urge Amarantha's adoption of—and to describe in passing—the newer mode: "Let it fly as unconfin'd/As its calm ravisher, the wind;/ . . . /Ev'ry tress must be confess'd/But neatly tangled at the best" (248, 5–6, 9–10; cf. 317, 2). The request cannot be, however, wholly ascribed to fashion; a venerable one, it is at least as old as Propertius. In poems on this subject, loose hair signifies the erotic; and Lovelace's words "ravisher" and "wanton," like his im-

agery of unconfinement, looseness, and of the man's curious eye
and hand flying about, suggest not merely fashions and hairstyles
but life style, moral choices. The erotic quality of flowing hair is
also evoked elsewhere: "When I lie tangled in her hair,/And fet-
ter'd to her eye" (284, 5–6); "Can trees be green [=innocent], and
to the air/Thus prostitute their flowing hair?" (307, 181–82).
These sensual overtones are not arbitrarily read into the text, for
the last three stanzas of "To Amarantha" describe, in fact, a sexual
encounter. Before the encounter, however, there is a stanza, in
which the poet uses hair to pay the usual compliment of comparing the lady to the sun and which has a last line that is one of
Lovelace's best:

> Do not then wind up that light
> In ribbands, and o'ercloud in night;
> Like the sun in's early ray,
> But shake your head and scatter day.
>   (248, 13–16)

The image of long, loose hair recurs in the pastoral and, most
memorably, in "Love Made in the First Age," in which a young
lady is seen in the setting of a primitive, simple life: "Each humble princess then did dwell/In the piazza of her hair" (329,
28–30).

Clothing has even more to do with erotic matters than do mirrors, dreams, hair. Like dreams, clothing is often used figuratively
in poetry. One such metaphor is common in connection with satire. Traditionally the satirist was he who stripped the veils of pre-
tence from men. Lovelace tells John Hall, "Thou . . . didst
whip/Upright the crooked age, and gilt Vice strip" (359, 13–14).
The idea is related to that of the "naked truth." Thus Heavenly
Love is pictured by Lovelace as undressed:

> And now a youth of more than godlike form
> Did th' inward minds of the dumb throng alarm;
> All nak'd, each part betray'd unto the eye,
> Chastely, for neither sex ow'd he or she.
> And this was Heavenly Love.
>   (346, 83–87)

Cupid's nakedness, on the other hand, has to do with bodily contact between lovers. Hence a dressed Cupid stands for moral decorum, as in Lovelace's praise of Fletcher's good taste:

> View here a loose thought said with such a grace,
> So well disguis'd, that 'twas conceiv'd by none
> But Cupid had Diana's linen on,
> And all his naked parts so veil'd.
>
> (272, 52–55)

The metaphor of clothing is used ingeniously in "La Bella Bona Roba." The speaker, contemning thin ladies—"I cannot tell who loves the skeleton/Of a poor marmoset, naught but bone, bone"— veers into a paradox: "Give me a nakedness with her clothes on" (296, 1–3). The nakedness is necessary, of course, for sex play; and the "clothes on" is either slang for skin—which is, after all, the dress of flesh—or the flesh itself, which, by long-standing tradition, was spoken of as the apparel of the soul. In short, the only clothing the lover wants on a woman is the metaphorical kind.[1] This viewpoint is also that of the persona of "The Fair Beggar," who, we saw, urges the beautiful woman to remove her ragged clothing so that he may cover her with his own body.

An attractive lady may not need apparel, but a lover is likely to try to prosper by finery. That attempt is the subject of an entire poem, "Strive Not." Informing the lover that sartorial dress is wrong both in itself and as strategy, the detached speaker uses various arguments to denigrate it. He, like Lear, reminds us that clothing is mainly stolen from the animals: "Strive not, vain lover, to be fine,/Thy silk's the silkworm's, and not thine" (312, 1–2; cf. 316, 16–18). The lover's ornate dress is, moreover, an insult to the intelligence of the lady he tries to impress thus; it reduces her to the level of one of Lovelace's favorite images, the trapped insect: "You lessen to a fly your mistress' thought,/To think it may be in a cobweb caught" (3–4). Continuing the insect imagery begun with "silkworm" and "fly," "cobweb" suggests the role of clothing vis-à-vis those whose hearts are captivated by it; not only does it come from the animals, but people whose affections are caught by it are rendered insect-like.

In a sudden turnabout, though, we find that the lover himself,

not the lady, has been foolishly trapped: "What though her thin
transparent lawn/Thy heart in a strong net hath drawn?" (5–6).
His finery now appears to be a belated attempt to retaliate, to
capture her heart by means of the very device of irresistible clothing which had caught him. He, not she, stands revealed as less-
ened to a fly; and his attempt to catch her seems doomed: for
"Not all the arms the God of Fire e'er made/Can the soft bul-
warks of nak'd Love invade" (7–8). This couplet contains a double entendre: following through upon the argument of the stanza,
it asserts that real, pure ("naked") love is not so superficial as to
be connected with external covering only, is in fact beyond clothing's power to arouse; it also refers to the fulfilment of love, the
sex act, which requires the discarding of dress.

Thence springs a third and conclusive argument to the case
against finery: it is irrelevant, indeed an obstacle, to the culmin-
ation of his love. "The gods go naked in their bliss" (298, 16).
After all, for battling with Cupid, the narrator of "The Duel"
stripped "naked all o'er, as he,/For so I was best arm'd, when
bare" (333, 19–20). We are thus reminded of the paradox that, in
order to achieve a physical consummation of love—a confronta-
tion of naked bodies—the lover and his lady first spend large
amounts of time, money, and effort in adorning themselves with
elegant apparel which will impress the other to the point of re-
moving his or her own.

Having reached so practical, elementary, and lubricous a tone,
the speaker resumes in the next stanza a high moral tack:

> Be truly fine, then, and yourself dress
> In her fair soul's immaculate glass:
> Then by reflection you may have the bliss
> Perhaps to see what a true fineness is.
>   (9–12)

"Dress," now spoken of metaphorically, means to polish, adorn,
set oneself in order. The lover's effort should go into developing
his character, into modeling himself upon her exemplary soul,
wherein her true beauty lies. The poem concludes by giving again
the second argument against ornate dress—that it bespeaks a low
mentality in the lady: "When all your gawderies will fit/Those

only that are poor in wit:/She that a clinquant [=glittering] outside doth adore,/Dotes on a gilded statue, and no more" (13–16). The man who resorts to finery is as silly as the woman who responds to it, for he lays bait for a woman who could as easily be impressed by a well-dressed statue or lout as by a man; after all, "Fools dote on satin motions [=marionets, puppets] lac'd" (298, 15). The merely well-dressed man is in fact not much different from a statue or "motion," both because of what he devotes his resources to and because of the kind of woman he seeks to catch, even as she, responding to a foppish man covered with tinsel, is herself a statue. Both get what they deserve. The poem is thus ultimately not only about clothing, despite frequent references to it, but about the proper way of mastering the lady and the right lady to choose in the first place—about the correct hierarchy of values. The lover is foolish for having fallen for the lady because of her finery, more foolish for thinking to catch her the same way, and most foolish for even desiring a woman who could be caught in this way.

The critique of clothing in "The Fair Beggar" is a mere masquerade for lascivious desires; in the "Strive Not" the criticism, limited to elaborate apparel, is a compound of tactful indecent suggestion and philosophic objections to finery. This antipathy to elegant dress seems elsewhere in Lovelace to be based wholly on philosophic grounds, on a rejection of the pretenses and veiling of civilized life. Clothing is but another form of imprisonment, entrapment. Such a feeling predominates in that genre traditionally averse to sophistication of all sorts, the pastoral. In "Aramantha," the young lady partakes, on rising, of none of the toiletries and rites of cosmetics that are *de rigueur* in society. She dons a simple dress,

> And puts on angry grey, whilst she,
> The envy of a deity,
> Arrays her limbs, too rich indeed
> To be enshrin'd in such a weed;
> Yet lovely 'twas, and strait, but fit,
> Not made for her, but she to it:
> By nature it sate close and free
> As the just bark unto the tree.
> (303, 7–14)

The idea that clothing should conform to the body and character
was to be fully developed by Thoreau in his perceptive and amusing assaults on fashion and dress in the first section of *Walden*.
The essence of Thoreau's thoughts is found in "Aramantha":

> All day imprison'd in a gown,
> . . . rack'd in silk 'stead of a dress,
> . . . clothed in a frame or press,
> And with that liberty and room
> The dead expatiate in a tomb
>   (16–20; cf. 317, 2)

In Lovelace's other revery of simplicity and the primitive life,
"Love Made in the First Age," the ideal young men and women
are depicted living either "Naked as their own innocence,/And
unembroider'd from offence/They went, above poor riches, gay"
(329, 43–45), or very nearly so: "Thus did they live; thus did they
love,/ . . . /And angels were, but with clothes on,/Which they
would put off cheerfully" (49, 51–52).

CHAPTER 8

Poetic Forms

I *Genres*

THOUGH a poet circumscribed in talent and sensibility, Lovelace worked in many verse forms. He abstained from the large statement—epic, drama (in his mature years), or philosophical or reflective poems; but he tried his hand with varying success at the smaller genres. The primary form of expression, for him as well as for his generation, was the lyric. A short poem conveying a mood or emotion, expressing a subjective outlook on life, delineating a solitary insight or perception, the lyric is often composed of stanzas—uniform within each poem—with varying line lengths and rhyme patterns. This definition covers poems as diverse as "To Althea," "The Grasshopper," "Gratiana singing and dancing," "The Scrutiny"—covers indeed the biggest and best part of Lovelace's output—for the lyric is an immensely flexible and receptive form.

One of the most popular poetic forms in the last decade of the sixteenth century was the sonnet. By Lovelace's time, it was in abeyance; when he gives several of his poems the title "sonnet," he intends the broader sense of the word, equivalent to "song," as in Donne's *Songs and Sonnets*. Similarly, though Lovelace labels various poems "ode" and "epode," he was probably not aware of the precise meaning of the terms. In varying stanza forms, these "odes" are simple love or occasional lyrics called "ode" because of the French adaptations of the casual Horatian ode. Some with intricate stanzas are superficially similar to Jonson's "odes" except that their rhyming lines are of equal length. Only the "Grasshopper" approximates the Classical Horatian ode in its moralizing, its meter, and its address to a persona.[1]

Some poems may be regarded either as part of a special subdivision of the lyric or as separate genres altogether. The elegy, for instance, laments the passing of a deceased person, celebrates his virtues and achievements, and seeks consolation in a set manner, be it pagan or Christian. Lovelace's elegies on the Princess Katherine, Mistress Filmer, and his own brother are limited in scope and depth. Where the elegy commemorates death, the epithalamium celebrates nuptials. For the wedding of the younger Charles Cotton, Lovelace wrote "The Triumphs of Philamore and Amoret." In rhyming couplets, instead of the complex stanza forms common in the genre, the poem also lacks the detailed description and lush last sections typical in such poetry. A related poem is on the occasion of the first anniversary of the wedding of his cousin, Thomas Stanley, the poet. If Spenser was the great model for subsequent writers of epithalamia, Donne was the master of anniversary poems; and Lovelace's bears the imprint of the master.

Two genres clearly distinct from the lyric are the pastoral and the satire. In Lovelace's time, one form looked to the past; the other, to the future. Though both bloomed in antiquity and revived in the late Middle Ages and the Renaissance, the pastoral in England had come into its own among the Elizabethans and, except in Milton's hands, was a slowly dying form thereafter; but the satire was the rising genre which would become the major form of poetic expression in the age from Dryden to Dr. Johnson. Lovelace's satire, examined in Chapter 4, is no mean achievement, albeit uneven in structure and quality; Lovelace's one pastoral, "Aramantha," is a curious work. Like the satire, with which it shares the distinction of being the longest of his works, as well as the only poem of its kind from his hand, and of appearing at the end of a volume of his poetry, it contains some of his best and worst lines. Each poem's best lines, however, differ radically from the other's; the pastoral contains lovely description of nature and the simple life, while the satire bites and whips.

Lovelace's pastoral owes less to the standard shepherds' dialogues and songs by Theocritus, Virgil, Spenser than to offshoots. For the pastoral encroached upon the drama and the romance-epic of the Renaissance. Tasso, for example, inserted a pastoral interlude in his epic *Jerusalem Delivered*. Erminia, anxious over the fate of her beloved Tancred in battle, leaves town dressed in armor. She is pursued by soldiers, loses her way, and finds shelter in a cottage on the Jordan River. Introduced to the simplicities and joys of pastoral life, she decides to remain with the shepherd and his wife. Book VII, v–xxii, describing Erminia's awakening

and initiation into pastoral life, closely parallels the first half of
"Aramantha," whose central figure is a young lady similarly fleeing to the simple world of nature from the wars and evils of the
world.

Lovelace's poem begins without any of the background story.
All we know is that day dawns for a beautiful young lady dwelling amid the simplicities of nature. Her dressing herself leads the
poet into what is a theme of the poem—and of all pastorals—the
contrast between the purity of the rustic life and the artificiality of
civilized society. Her toilet involves a simple dip of her face in a
pail of water, not the long rites of pride with countless cosmetics
and paints whose purpose is to falsify a woman's appearance:

> No cabinets with curious washes,
> Bladders, and perfumed plashes,
> No venom-temper'd water's here,
> Mercury is banished this sphere.
>
> . . . .
> Far hence all Iberian smells,
> Hot amulets, pomander spells;
> Fragrant gales, cool air, the fresh
> And natural odour of her flesh
> Proclaim her sweet from th' womb, as morn.
> Those colour'd things were made not born,
> Which, fix'd within their narrow straits,
> Do look like their own counterfeits.
> (303, 21–24, 27–34)

Leaving her abode, she enters a garden, where the flowers offer
themselves to her. She moves on from the garden to a meadow,
where the cattle offer her adulation—and breakfast: "Begging her
charitable leisure/To strip them of their milky treasure" (87–88).
Here again follows a brief sermon on the contrast between nature
and society: the heroine regrets that the cows who so graciously
give man milk are rudely slaughtered for food. After her meal, she
goes to a wood stream; and now the fish are responsive to femi-
nine pulchritude. The birds serve too:

> Where th' winged music of the air
> Do richly feast, and for their fare,

> Each evening in a silent shade,
> Bestow a grateful serenade.
>   (161–64)

Having arduously spent the day being worshipped by vegetable, animal, fish, and fowl, she drifts off to sleep amid echoes of the Marvellian Garden. At this point, the description ends of her solitary idyll, which constitutes the first half of the poem.

Now dramatic and amatory matter comes to the fore. She awakens to the sound of a man's lamenting the loss of his beloved. When he utters the name Lucasta, the heroine smiles and from behind a bush urges him to tell his story, for "To show our wound is half to heal" (234). He relates that the Druids killed Lucasta. When she uses contemptuous language about Lucasta, he is about to fight her but discovers that Aramantha is his Lucasta. She,

> With a soft lip and gentle eye,
> Then closes with him on the ground;
> And now her smiles have heal'd his wound,
> Alexis too again is found.
> But not until those heavy crimes
> She hath kiss'd off a thousand times.
>   (311–16)

Alexis is a name used elsewhere in Lovelace's poems in a manner to suggest that it applies to the poet himself, but the man's lapse, like that of Byron's Manfred, remains unnamed. Instead, the background of the story is sketched, a tale of adventures quite like those encountered by the characters of romance-epic, a tale which also seems to allude to the recent political turmoil. Alexis converts to the simplicities of pastoral existence; and they live thus out their days, married in nature.

Pastorals have not been in favor as a means of expression for two hundred and fifty years; to read such works sympathetically requires, therefore, a considerable effort of the imagination. We learn eventually to see the beauty of some by Theocritus, Virgil, and Milton; but most pastorals, Lovelace's included, remain lifeless. Surely, the second half, with its disguises, its "another part of the forest" coincidences, its vague sentiments and ridiculous turns of events, has not advanced the art of the genre any. The first half of the poem, however, contains—if we except the admitted bathos of Aramantha's "breakfast on the teat" of the divinely descended and solicitous cow—some lovely descriptive passages befitting an idyll. The simple life amid the flowers and birds of garden and wood is described in limpid octosyllabics which are nearly on a par with the contemporary "Garden" and "Bermudas" of Marvell and which look ahead to Milton's idyll of Adam and Eve in paradise.

II *Prosody, Syntax, Organization*

The great ages of English lyric poetry, most notably the early seventeenth century, developed varied and complex stanza forms. Men like Donne and Herbert showed resourcefulness in inventing a different stanza for nearly every lyric and in adhering to the form throughout the poem. In such matters, Lovelace was quite their equal. In all, his poetry contains forty-eight different stanza forms—thirty, or just two thirds, of them in the 1649 volume.

These range all the way from such simple ones as *10a 10a 10a* and *7a 8a 7b 8b* to the large fourteen-line stanza of "A Mock Song." Of the forty-eight forms, five are used in more than one poem and in both the 1649 and 1659 volumes, two in more than two poems. Of those once repeated, the eminently successful are *8a 8b 8a 8b 8c 8c* ("The Fair Beggar," "In Mine Own") and *8a 8a 8b 8c 8c 8b* ("Gratiana singing and dancing," "Love Made in the First Age"). Used five times is the ballad-like *8a 6b 8a 6b*, which achieved greatness in the "Wars," and *8a 8a 8b 8b*, consisting in effect of octosyllabic couplets divided typographically into stanzas, used to good effect in "A Fly . . . Claret." Two poems, "Lucasta Laughing" and "A Black Patch," are examples of free-form single stanzas whose irregular mixture of short and long rhyming lines are typical of what a few years later would be written by Cowley and others as "Pindarics" or "Pindarique Odes." The "Ode Lyric. To Lucasta" is a sport of six and seven syllable lines in mono-rhymed stanzas of four or five lines.

Of the one hundred and three original poems by Lovelace, sixty-three, or two-thirds, are in stanzaic forms; the remaining forty, in couplets. The latter consist of two heptasyllabic poems; single poems in six, nine, and twelve syllable forms; thirteen poems, including some of his best, in the octosyllabic which had become popular in Lovelace's time and was perfected by Marvell; and

twenty poems in the iambic pentameter couplet which is the
basic, most frequently used English verse form. At a glance the
statistics are:[2]

	1649 (60 poems)	1659 (43 poems)
Couplet poems	20	20
Stanzaic poems	39 (+1)	21 (+2)
(Stanza forms)	(30)	(18)

This table shows that, while the number of couplet poems remained exactly the same, Lovelace's ingenuity in inventing new
stanza forms diminished.

Lovelace's syntax is sometimes contorted and obscure, perhaps
unduly so for even his period. It may take us some time to see that
the stanza,

> Night as clear Hesper shall our tapers whip
> From the light casements where we play,
> And the dark hag from her black mantle strip,
> And stick there everlasting day,
> (260, 33–36)

means "our tapers, in the guise of Hesperus, or as clear as Hesperus shines at day's end, shall whip night from the casements,
. . . strip the black mantle from the dark hag, and stick in its
place everlasting day." Sometimes the verb is tucked in at the
end: "If Pliny, Lord High Treasurer of all/Nature's exchequer
shuffled in this our ball,/Painture, her richer rival, did admire"
(351, 1–3) reads "if Pliny—Lord High Treasurer of all Nature's
treasury which is shuffled in this planet—did admire painting, Nature's richest rival [in that it goes beyond nature]." The omission
of the relative pronoun, a device common in his time, does not
help us to unfold involuted constructions, as in "But I shall leave
him till a nag on/He gets to prosecute the dragon" (286, 37–38);
for the modern reading would be "till he gets a nag on which to
prosecute." The lines "Twere better, heavy one, to crawl/Forgot,
than, raised, trod on fall" (331, 23–24) may mean "better to crawl
forgotten than to be exalted [by an undeserved poem] only to be
trodden on and cast down."

Some constructions remain insoluble. Does "Up with the day,

the sun thou welcom'st then,/ . . . /And all these merry days
mak'st merry men,/Thyself, and melancholy streams" (259, 9,
11–12) mean that the grasshopper makes men, itself, and even
melancholy streams happy, or that it makes men and itself happy
while the melancholy streams (flows) away? In the stanza,

> There quench my heat, and thou shalt sup
>   Worthy the lips that it must touch;
> Nectar from out the starry cup,
>   I beg thy breath not half so much,
>   (298, 19–22)

if the third line is syntactically interchangeable with the second
and looks back to what the lady will sup on his lips, that is, something delicious, the fourth line becomes then the "ungallant" suggestion that the woman is more desirous of sexual intercourse than
is the man. Or, with punctuation uncertain, the third line may be
the other half of a highly contorted comparison begun in the following line: "I do not beg nectar from the starry cup half as much
as I beg your breath." This construction seems an improbable one,
but with Lovelace we cannot be sure.

Some conclusions to the poems are obscure or, while half clear
in themselves, are cryptic with reference to the rest of the poems,
as in "Calling Lucasta" or "Aramantha,"

> Ye panting virgins, that do meet
> Your loves within their winding-sheet,
> Breathing and constant still ev'n there;
> Or souls their bodies in yon' sphere,
> Or angels men return'd from hell,
> And separated minds can tell.
>   (311, 379–84)

Sometimes the opening may be troublesome:

> As I beheld a winter's evening air,
> Curl'd in her court false locks of living hair,
> Butter'd with jessamine the sun left there,
>
> Galliard and clinquant she appear'd to give,
> A serenade or ball to us that grieve,
> And teach us *à la mode* more gently live.
>   (317, 1–6)

Some obscurities stem from the use of a language now defunct, like
the heraldic symbolism in the second stanza of the "Mock Song";
others from allusions to current events, like, "Write a deep epic
poem, and you may/As soon delight them as the opera,/Where
they Diogenes thought in his tub/Never so sour did look, so sweet
a club" (361, 57–60), which E. E. Duncan-Jones has shown to be
perfectly intelligible—if we know of a cluster of trivial incidents
on the contemporary literary scene.[3]

In short, some of the difficulties in Lovelace's poetry—of which
there are a considerable number—are due to his sloppiness, his
topicality, his dilettantish dabbling in the art; others are deliberate, the sort of complicated construction and obscure references
conventional in the separate traditions of metaphysical poetry and
Juvenalian satire. But we must not overemphasize Lovelace's
amateur status or his supposed indifference to the polish of his
verses. A lazy poet would have contented himself with writing in
couplets instead of taking the trouble to invent so many different
stanza forms. Furthermore, to Wilkinson's findings that the dedicatory poems Lovelace wrote for others' books were revised when
printed in his own books and that some corrections were even
made while the book was in the press, Willa Evans's researches
into manuscript material have added additional evidence of Lovelace's care and meaningful revision in the direction of greater
clarity.[4]

As for the order of the poems in the printed volumes, no clear
design is discernible, The opening nine lyrics (exclusive of the
dedication) of the 1649 volume cover, in stanzaic form, the spectrum of love but hop about without any pattern. First come two
great songs of courtly love and honor, "To . . . Seas" and "To
. . .Wars"; then in "A Paradox," which follows, we find the
world of inconstancy. The "To . . . Hair" begins with a polite
paean to the lady's beauty and concludes with sexual delights and
scabrous allusions. The Petrarchan unrequited love lament, "To
Chloe," is followed by the Donnean seduction poem, "Depose."
Two courtly poems lavishing praise on the beauty and attractive
powers of the lady, "The Rose" and "Gratiana singing and dancing," are succeeded by the worldly, cynical "Scrutiny."

Despite their thematic heterogeneity, these poems have one
stylistic quality in common: their excellence. Beautifully, sometimes perfectly, constructed, they contain memorable individual

lines, images, strokes of logic or sophistry. Taking note perhaps of the importance of first and last impressions, Lovelace placed these nine poems—which he himself may have considered his best—at the beginning of the volume and rounded it out with "Aramantha." As with the nine, circumstantial evidence indicates that he, or his publisher, thought highly of that pastoral. It was separately referred to in the title of the book and separately paginated.

After the "Scrutiny," a pair of occasional poems in pentameter couplets relate to the royal family. From then on, it is hard to find any common denominator. Anecdotes of Cupid; dialogues between lovers or friends; Epicurean drinking songs; seduction and inconstancy poems; prison poems; elegies; poems praising the beauty of the mistress; occasional poems thanking his hosts Ellinda, A.L., Amyntor, or introducing plays, books, paintings; dramatic monologues; answer poems; poems of Petrarchan lament; and advice poems to Petrarchan lover or bereaved brother—all appear in no discernible order. Their forms are equally varied and helter skelter, the couplet appearing mainly in the occasional and dedicatory poems, in the dramatic monologues, and in the pastoral.

The 1659 posthumous volume contains only two-thirds as many poems. In it we find more of an attempt at design, but Lovelace is unlikely to have had anything to do with it and, furthermore, such pattern as exists is without deep significance. Broadly speaking, there are three different clusters of poems. The first dozen, in stanzaic form, are mainly Petrarchan, telling of Lucasta's attractions and powers over men. The second group consists generally of a dozen or so poems in octosyllabics on insect, birds, and small creatures; this cluster is inexplicably interrupted, in the very middle, by a half dozen stanzaic love poems. The last group comprises a dozen occasional poems in rhyming couplets, mainly pentameter, addressed to friends on their painting, literary works, weddings, anniversaries. Whether or not the first dozen stanzaic love poems of this volume are meant to correspond in some way to the first nine of the earlier volume, the closing "On Sannazar" certainly corresponds to the closing "Aramantha." In either case, Lovelace makes his one attempt in a venerable Renaissance genre and at a large statement, writes his longest—albeit not wholly successful—poem, and strikes off some of his best lines.

It has been the universal opinion of critics and scholars during

the hundred and fifty years in which the entire Lovelace output
has been before the public that the 1659 volume has almost nothing of value. This judgment is, however, unfair. The best known,
to be sure, of Lovelace's poems, as well as many merely fine things,
are in the first volume. But, without the posthumous volume, we
would be deprived of the duel poems and of the whole genre of
insect and creature poems—principally the "Ant," "Snail," and
two fly lyrics—which is one of Lovelace's contributions to English
literature and of which he had not given a sign in 1649. Among
the love poems we would be without the "Strive Not," "In Allusion," "Cupid Far Gone," "The Black Patch," "You Are Deceived,"
not to speak of the excellent drinking song, the second "Loose
Saraband," the dreamlike "Love Made in the First Age," and the
biting satires, "Mock Song" and "On Sannazar." Though the love
poetry of the second volume is inferior, this collection is more
endowed with a commodity Lovelace is not wealthy in—a sense
of humor, as is evident in the insect poems and in the "Cupid Far
Gone" and "Strive Not."

Fruitless as it is to go into lengthy comparisons, were one yet to
make a breakdown of the poems by quality—admittedly a subjective matter—the results,

	1649	*1659*
Perfect	6	0
Very good	5	7
Good	12	12

would show that, while the best poems are in the earlier volume,
the number of merely good poems is as high in 1659 as in 1649,
and the proportion is even larger. With such novelty in subject
matter, levity, and balance of treatment, we must conclude—if all
the poems in the 1659 volume represent in fact his later work and
are not merely the omnium-gatherum of pieces omitted in 1649—
that Lovelace was beginning to strike out into new directions at
the time of his death at the age of thirty-nine.

CHAPTER 9

Influences and Parallels

I *Lovelace's Place*

TO ASCERTAIN Lovelace's place on the poetic map, we must take account of the common classification of English poets of 1600–1660 into four groups. Least important were the Spenserians, who were conservative in technique and in outlook. A second group were the Sons of Ben, who followed, in varying degrees, Jonson's self-conscious, deliberate program of reforming English poetry by casting out the hyperbole, sensuousness, sentimentality, surfeit of conceit, and excess of Elizabethan rhetoric and Petrarchan paradoxes and by bringing to bear on English verse the succinctness, polish, urbanity, moderation, moral tone, and calm pagan outlook of the ancient lyric poet—the tone of the gentleman in poetry.

The followers of Donne, constituting the third and fourth groups, were devoted to the master's own sort of reform in English poetry. Like Jonson, Donne turned his back on the Elizabethan style and poetic diction; but, instead of taking the Classical way as an alternative, Donne substituted a personal style that was colloquial and dramatic; in its fidelity to the twists and turns of the thinking mind, it favored the harsh and direct over the "poetic" and polished. Taking imagery where he found it—which meant, because of his "hydroptique" curiosity and voracious reading, from almost everywhere—he wrote poems which struck a new note of vitality, psychological realism, and satiric irony. Donne ransacks the fields of philosophy and the new science; Jonson, the Classics.

The third group consists of Donne's followers working in the secular line (Lord Herbert, Suckling, Carew, Marvell, Cleveland); and the fourth, of those in the religious (George Herbert, Vaughan, Crashaw). Donne was so powerful and far-ranging a poet that what he had handled in the course of a brief career, it seemed, could only be taken up and developed piecemeal by

145

others. Each follower specialized in one aspect of the master's art.

Where does Lovelace stand? He has little to do with the Spenserians, for neither his pastoral nor his pastoral-like dialogues have any of their cloying sweetness and moral emphasis. Nor does he share anything with the religious metaphysicals. There are signs, however, of connections with the Sons of Ben. When at his best, he evinces something of the Jonsonian coolness and polish. Like Jonson, he translated from Catullus and the later poets of antiquity; the influence of the *Greek Anthology*, especially in his use of the Cupid anecdotes, suggests proximity to Jonson and, even more, to that "Son of Ben," Herrick.

Lovelace seems closest to the secular Donne followers by his use of conceits, by the occasional harshness and obscurity of his style. His affiliations, though, can be seen to best advantage by considering him as a member of a fifth school, or a sub-group of the seculars—the "Cavaliers." These were the poets loosely connected with the court of Charles I, men of the 1630's and 1640's—Carew, Suckling, Cartwright, Randolph—and, peripherally, men not at court but influenced by its style: Marvell, Herrick, Waller, the early Vaughan. Moving on terms of intimacy with the highest born of the land, they provided much of the intellectual fare of the king and his courtiers. They set the literary tone of the court. Written for a small aristocratic circle, "Cavalier poetry" expresses the ideals and values of its limited audience; but this poetry is open to contemporary fashions as well as Classical influences.

Mainly amatory—at times, expressing the courtly and "platonic" sentiments fashionable among the French-born Queen Henrietta Maria and her ladies; at other times, reflecting the earthy and ribald outlook of the young courtier, university wit, man of the world—this poetry evokes a picture of the courtier, fully rounded in the best Renaissance manner. But ribald or gallant, the Cavaliers have an air of civilized grace and elegance; mixing sophistication with naïveté and obscenity, they are rarely vulgar. In their devotion to great numbers of women, these poets carry on the aspirations of the persona of Donne's early lyrics, just as their earthiness, dialectic of passion, occasional use of conceits, hardness of line, and cultivated colloquial rhythms are in the Donne manner. They show deftness, spontaneity, even a roughness which is partly assumed. They write a masculine poetry that is vigorous, charming, uninhibited, full of sensitivity, curiosity, skepticism, moral candor.

Yet the Cavalier poets have also their weak side. Open to many experiences, they often deal with superficialities rather than with the great themes. Their own distinct contribution is, as Skelton says, "their enjoyment of the casual, the amateur, the affectionate poetry written by the way," their celebration of the minor pleasures of life.[1] Despite dramatic openings and a knowing air, the Cavaliers strike attitudes rather than open new areas of feeling. They lack a serious moral fiber. More detached and courtly than Donne the intellectual, they simplify his rhetoric and rhythmic effects, pare down his erudition, while reviving some of the sensuous style, as well as the lover's beseechings and the catalogues of the lady's beauties, of the Elizabethans. Next to Donne's work, their poetry seems less passionate and more civilized, or degenerate into frivolity or sexual cynicism. They write, besides occasional poetry, short lyrics mainly of love of women and sometimes love of God. Not striving for greatness, they are successful within their scope, and they produce the most delicate lyrics of the century. Gay, gallant, graceful songs is their goal, and their achievement of it justifies their work. For more than that they have no time or ability.

The Cavaliers may be regarded, therefore, as a subgroup of the secular Donne followers, which discards some of the more abrasive metaphysical way of writing—though not the scabrous content of Donne's poems—for a style at once more courtly and comprehensive, more open to the influence, however indirect, of Jonson. Reducing the range of imagery, the Cavaliers produce persuasive discourse and smooth rhythms with careless ease. Leaning in content to Donne and in form to Jonson, combining passion, exuberance, intellectual imagery, dialectical method, imaginative elaboration with discipline, tact, Classical neatness and point, the Cavaliers exist at the juncture in sensibility of the secular Donne followers and the Sons of Ben, with a leavening of the influence of Greek and Latin lyrists, and Continental Petrarchan and libertine currents.

II *Classical Influences*

The Classical literature Lovelace imbibed as part of the Renaissance gentleman's education made an appreciable impression on him. He was the only one of the leading Cavaliers to translate from the Classics. Some forty poems in all, the translations are mainly of minor Latin figures, except for a dozen poems of Catullus and a half dozen each by Martial and Ausonius. Lovelace was the first in England to make a literal version of Catullus's terse lyrics to Lesbia. A student of Catullus's influence, J. B. Emperor, finds Lovelace's choices incomprehensible: they are not of the popular "sparrow," "kisses," or *vivamus* lyrics but include a poem of mournful recrimination, a half intelligible pederastic epigram, or a vulgar outcry against brothel madams.[2]

The giants—Homer and Virgil, Sappho and Lucretius—seem, like the later giants, Shakespeare and Spenser, not to have interested Lovelace. But the love elegists hover over the "original" matter written by him and by those who influenced him. Juvenal and Martial likewise stimulated him, but undoubtedly the one ancient poet most influential on Lovelace was Horace. He is responsible for the substance of nearly the whole of the "Advice," with its argument against ambitious travel over dangerous seas to distant places and with its philosophy of the golden mean (*Satires*, I, i; *Odes*, II, x; *Epistles*, I, i); for the core of "The Ant," the insect presented in *Satires* I, i, as an example of the prudent, provident creature; for the second half of "The Grasshopper," with its praise of epicurean retreat amid duress, and for "Amyntor's Grove," with its description of such of life (*Epodes*, ii, xiii; *Odes*, I, xvii; II, xviii). Lovelace also owes a debt to Horace for "To Lucasta. From Prison," with its cloying apotheosis of the sovereign (*Odes*, I, ii); for the freedom and confinement theme (*Odes*, I, xxii), for the vituperations in "I Did Believe" and "You Are Deceived" against ugly women (*Epodes*, viii, xii); for the description in "On Sannazar" of the unsettled relations of poet and patron or audience (*Epistles*, I, xviii, xix); for the poem exhorting brother Francis not to mourn (*Odes*, II, ix).

Another important ancient influence was the *Greek Anthology*, especially the amatory poems of Meleager. These contained, as did the Latin love elegies, many anecdotes about Cupid and

Venus which allegorically describe the love experience and were translated by, among others, Jonson and Herrick. Similarity of theme connect Lovelace's "A Black Patch" and V, 163; "Love Enthroned" and V, 177; "The Duel" and V, 179; "Loose Saraband [1649]" and V, 214.

Cupid is also prominent in the *Anacreontea,* a pseudonymous Greek work of late antiquity. "Loose Saraband [1659]" recalls the theme of XLIX; "The Duel" is a paraphrase of XIII; "A Fly . . . Claret" may be based on VI, as well as on IX, 749 of the *Anthology.* Lovelace is most indebted to pseudo-Anacreon in the first part of "The Grasshopper," which captures the geniality and verve of poem XXXIV. Lovelace's version is longer, more detailed and "conceited," and adds a melancholy lesson—the sudden death in winter. Because of his change to the Horatian manner midway in the poem, it is a curious example of the fusion of two different Classical genres. Over a dozen poems on singing locusts and cicadas, drunk with dew, were written as well by Meleager and others in the *Anthology* (VII, 189–201; IX, 92).

Lovelace's work evinces no signs of any acquaintance with Medieval writers and only few with the early, High Renaissance writers. He must have been aware of the Latinists Sarbiewski and Secundus, and of Tasso's *Aminta* and *Jerusalem Delivered.* Recent research has suggested familiarity—if only through the translations of Stanley and Sherburne—with the work of late Renaissance Continental writers like the French Theophile, St. Amant, Tristan l'Hermit, Voiture, Brignole-Sale, de Malleville; the Italian Guarini, Achillini, Marino and his followers; the Spaniard Quevedo. Even though Lovelace exhibits none of his friend Suckling's interest in Shakespeare, some tenuous parallels and echoes exist.[3]

III *Donne and Lovelace*

Unquestionably the single most pervasive influence on Lovelace was that of Donne. Though Lovelace was by temperament courtly and serious, various of his themes and entire poems would not exist had it not been for the presence of the libertine love verses of the 1590's. Even poems substantively unlike Donne bear his trademark in structure, turn of phrase, image, sophistry, or title. In the "Grasshopper," for example, the poet has been speak-

ing of the insect's happy existence destroyed by the coming of
winter. Amidst this calm moral tone and this observation of nature which has kinship with late Greek poetry and none with
Donne, the poet suddenly apostrophizes the victimized insect,
"poor verdant fool, and now green ice!" Like the later "Aetna in
epitome," "green ice" is, although not directly comparable to anything in Donne, a metaphysical, fantastic touch made possible by
Donne's manner.

A good dozen lyrics are clearly modelled on poems or themes of
Donne's. In "To . . . Seas," the master can be felt everywhere.
The theme is Donne's famous assertion of mutual, faithful love's
surviving the temporary parting of the lovers (cf. "Song. Sweetest
Love," "The Valediction: Forbidding Mourning," Elegy XVI).
The dramatic situation is, as in Donne's "Dream" or "Flea,"
graphic; the lover addresses the lady in such a way that we can
readily visualize the weeping woman and the confident, earnest
man. Lovelace's mock use of Petrarchan sighs-tears and wind-sea,
like his conjunction of earthly love with religious imagery, is in the
manner of Donne's "Canonization"; the dangers of sea crossing is
touched on by Donne in his parting poems as well as in the
"Hymn to Christ." The closely reasoned, overt syllogistic form—
enhancing rather than detracting from the lyric quality—recalls
Donne; the logical roadsigns are in evidence at the beginning of
the lines and stanzas: "If. . . . Then. . . . But. . . . For. . . .
Though. . . . So then. . . ." Finally, the idea of the lovers' souls
greeting like angels and anticipating the heavenly union is close to
the argument of poems like the "Extasie." "To . . . Seas," then, is
a pastiche of Donne themes, images, methods. Derivative, the
poem is yet well wrought, musical; it persuades and sings. In this
instance, Donne clearly taught Lovelace how to write and think,
if not how to woo.

In "The Flea," Donne taught Lovelace how to seduce as well,
for "Depose" is likewise an "approach" filled with sophistry. In
either case, the lover and his lady stand to each other as does a
teacher carrying out an experiment before a pupil and applying
a moral lesson. The closing themes are nearly the same:

> So then enrich me with that treasure
> Will but increase your store.
>   (249, 7–8)

> Just so much honor, when thou yield'st to me,
> Will waste, as this flea's death took life from thee.
>   ("The Flea")

Lovelace has actually improved on Donne in that his central image of the ring has, as we have noted, an obvious sexual significance—compare "at's own mother he [Cupid] is offering,/His finger now fits any ring" (333, 7–8)—which the flea has not. The elder's poem is nevertheless more dramatic, its ratiocination more thorough, its ramifications pursued relentlessly. "The Flea" is a playlet in three scenes, acted out in soliloquy, while Lovelace's poem remains a slyly lascivious analogy or demonstration that is more epigrammatic than dramatic.

Donne's "Flea" and "Dream" are models of construction for even such a lyric as Lovelace's "A Fly . . . Claret," which has nothing to do with Donne in either content or theme. All three are dramatic monologues which sketch a little play with changing actions and responses, with implied debate and evident sophistry. The remarks of the only speaker conjure up the scene, the auditor, the advancing action, and the resolution. The abrupt turnabout at the end is in the manner of Donne's poetry.

"The Scrutiny" is Donnean in its very title, which, like "The Indifferent" or "Communitie," radiates ambiguity and ironic succinctness. No "she," we are assured, is neglected for sexual examination by the persona. The structure adheres, as Alvarez suggests, to the pattern established in such Donne lyrics as "The Good Morrow": beginning with a personal question concerning the emotions, the persona answers it with a show of logic and conceits, and ends on a dialectical and emotional point of rest.[4] The flippant manner of the hard-boiled libertine, speaking in a sort of mock outrage and half believing his own excuses and ironic claims, derives from Donne's seduction and inconstancy poems and from lines like "Now though hast lov'd me one whole day," "He is stark mad, who ever says,/That he hath been in love an hour." Signally close is Donne's "The Indifferent," in which appear phrases like "fair and brown," "variety," "let me, and do you, twenty know."

Another seduction lyric, "Love . . . First Age," is, we saw, an exercise in libertinism which owes not a little to Donne's Elegy XVII, "Variety," notably to lines in it like

How happy were our Syres in ancient time,
Who held plurality of loves no crime!
Women were then no sooner asked than won,
And what they did was honest and well done.

The opening of "La Bella Bona Roba," has that Donnean worldly
confident tone, colloquial ease, terseness in mirroring thought—
"naught but bone, bone." The burly voice expressing its taste—
"Give me a nakedness with her clothes on/ . . . Pass rascal deer,
strike me the largest doe" (296, 3, 15)—is like the voice in "The
Indifferent." Effective as well is the "metaphysical shudder," the
perception of the skeleton behind the beautiful face, the remem-
brance of death in the midst of erotic attraction, as in Donne's
"bracelet of bright hair about the bone."

Lovelace's "An Anniversary . . . Stanley, Esquire" is likewise
immersed in the master's method of expression. The sun is addressed by the poet in an irreverent manner reminiscent of
Donne's "Busy old fool, unruly Sun" and "ride ten thousand days
and nights": "Be witness then, all-seeing Sun,/Old spy, thou that
thy race hast run/In full five thousand rings" (350, 19–21).
Donne's "Our eye-beams twisted" is behind "Hast thou beheld a
pair/Twist their soft beams like these . . . ?" (12–13).

In Lovelace's "Love Conquered," Cupid is offended by a
couple's fidelity; in Donne's "The Indifferent," Venus takes um-
brage at a few constant lovers. "The Apostacy" deals, like Donne's
"Goe and Catch," with the difficulty of finding a constant woman
and utilizes a similar irony and a listing of impossibilities, which
is reminiscent as well of Donne's "The Will."

The influence of Donne is apparent not only in the theme and
structure of entire poems; the mixture of long and very short lines
is typical of him and of his followers like Herbert and Vaughan,
as is the emphasis on compactness, sophistry, and conceits rather
than on lush description of the beauty of the beloved. A thought
like "There's not a virtuous she in all the world" (333, 24) is part
of the cynical outlook naturalized by the master. The conceited
manner of Lovelace's "The Muff" reminded one critic of Donne's
"Flea," but missing are the unity and the effectiveness of the older
poem; in the last stanza, though, we recognize more clearly the
virile assertiveness that is the Donne tone: "Lay-lovers," "I, in my
invention tough." Conversely, a certain manly tenderness in the

"Dialogue" of Lucasta and Alexis, on parting, "It is a swounding
for a while from bliss,/Till kind 'How do you?' calls us from the
fit" (260, 3–4), recalls the master: "Think that we/Are but turned
aside to sleep." Or, in the same Lovelace poem, "Shadows no
longer than the sun remain,/But when his beams, that made 'em,
fly, they fly" (19–20), is based on Donne's "A Lecture Upon the
Shadow."

Miscellaneous echoes include Lovelace's "And now like some
pale ghost I walk,/And with another's spirit talk" (330, 5–6) and
Donne's "I long to talk with some old lover's ghost" and the setting of "The Apparition"; Lovelace's "his fair murd'ress" and
Donne's "O murdress"; Lovelace's "honour, the fool's giant" (325,
42) and Donne's "th' enormous Gyant, your Disdaine,/And . . .
th' enchantress Honor"; Lovelace's "Austere and Cynic!" (321,
19) and Donne's "Rebel and Atheist!"; Lovelace's "Off with that
crowned Venice [=highly prized glass; adornment]" (324, 9) and
Donne's "Off with that Girdle"; Lovelace's "I'll cover thee with
mine own self" (298, 30) and Donne's "What needs thou have
more covering than a man?"; Lovelace's "She that a clinquant
outside doth adore,/Dotes on a gilded statue, and no more" (313,
15–16) and Donne's "But he who loveliness within/Hath found,
all outward loathes,/For he who colour loves, and skinne,/Loves
but their oldest clothes"; Lovelace's "But shake your head and
scatter day" (248, 16) and Donne's "the sun-beames of her hair";
Lovelace's "Then understand you not, fair choice,/This language
without tongue or voice?" (313, 1–2) and Donne's "Thou didst not
understand/The mystique language of the eye nor hand."

Some of the nature lore that interested Lovelace was used earlier by Donne: "As he that sees a star fall, runs apace,/And finds a
jelly in the place," "As an amber enwraps a Bee," "Meethinks all
Cities now, but Anthills bee/Where . . . the several laborers I
see,/ . . . They're but Ants," "Fish chaseth fish . . ./And is it of
necessity/That thousand guiltless smalls, to make one great, must
die?"

We must recognize, of course, that some of these parallels may
well be examples of the adoption by both poets independently of
images conventional in the Renaissance rather than of Donne's
inventing a conceit and Lovelace's imitating it. But even these
commonplaces often have a liveliness characteristic of Donne's re-
juvenation of clichés and imitated by Lovelace. Another thing to

be remarked is that, influenced as he is by Donne, Lovelace often responds only to the surface: he seizes the technique but not the feeling. He reproduces the sophistry, the lover's "lines," some of the themes, especially the cynical and bawdy ones, the dramatic construction and colloquial language, the images, ideas and whole poems sometimes; but he does so without the depth, the learning, the range of moods. Lovelace does solemnly what Donne often did with malice and mockery. He captures, in short, the superficial fireworks, the audible sounds instead of the subtle overtones and insights. Donne's rendering visible the invisible—the "Bracelet of bright hair about the bone," for example, reminds us of the transience, vanity, and poignance of human love—is achieved by Lovelace only spasmodically. On the other hand, though his style is marred by ill-digested Donnean ideas and conceits, he occasionally manages to avoid the excesses and abstruseness of a Cowley or a Cleveland.

IV *Contemporaries and Successors*

With his friend Suckling, Lovelace shares many things, the most notable being the anti-Petrarchan poems of counsel, as in Suckling's "Why So Pale and Wan" and Lovelaces's "Strive Not"— though the latter is modeled in part also on the "against finery" genre from Propertius to Jonson and Herrick. Suckling says in effect to the lover, "Why shed your Petrarchan tears, if she will not be moved by them; besides, if she will not respond to you at your best, without tears, the devil might as well have her." Lovelace says, "Why dress up so elegantly if she will not be moved by that and if, furthermore, were she to be attracted merely by such apparel, she would be so foolish as consequently not to be desirable in the first place."

With Carew, the most interesting of many parallels is "A Fly that flew into my Mistress her eye" which recalls not only Lovelace's several poems on the difficulties of a fly's life but also the one of the similar death of the bee and the resultant black patch. Even closer to the latter is Carew's "Upon a Mole in Celia's bosom." C. F. Williamson remarks that despite verbal parallels ("phoenix," "spices," "aromatic," "sweat," "paradise"), the two lyrics differ in a manner characteristic of their creators. Carew's version is sensual in atmosphere and description—a mole on the breast rather than on the face. His poem has more force and balance by confining itself to two conceits, while Lovelace sets off a shower of them. Williamson concludes that Lovelace borrowed the idea from Carew, diluted it with characteristic inferiority of technique, and exhausted his ingenuity in the central passage, so that the end, unlike Carew's, is anticlimactic and feeble.[5]

One of the religious metaphysicals, George Herbert is a poet whose influence we would not expect to see in Lovelace because Herbert published only devotional poetry; Lovelace, secular. Yet there are a half-dozen suggestive echoes. The influence of Jonson and his followers, more a matter of spirit and lapidary style than of specific images and themes, is harder to trace. A characteristic example of Jonson's adoption of the late Greek and Latin anecdotes of Cupid is his "Dream," but Lovelace's numerous lyrics of this sort are closer to Herrick, who more than any other English poet translated, paraphrased, adapted this genre. With the minor poets of his own generation who responded to both Donne and Jonson—William Habington, William Cartwright, Thomas Randolph, Thomas Stanley, William Hammond, Francis Kynaston, John Hall, Abraham Cowley, John Cleveland, Edmund Waller—Lovelace likewise shares many themes, interests, images and lines. But of all his contemporaries, he was closest to Andrew Marvell.

Marvell and Lovelace were acquaintances, probably as early as 1637, at Cambridge. Lovelace, as the elder and the one with higher social standing, no doubt was mentor to Marvell and helped him come in contact with the court circle, encouraged his talent, and exercised an influence on his style. L. N. Wall suggests, in a note on Marvell's sources, that Marvell's forte, the smoothly flowing octosyllabics, were in part "imitations" of, improvements on, Lovelace's common use of that meter. Individual poems show also mutual influences in substance: Lovelace's "Aramantha" pastoral resembles Marvell's "Upon Appleton House" in theme, structure, as well as meter. Both poems deal with retirement in time of civil war. The persona of the Marvell poem walks through gardens, meadow, river, communes with birds, and confronts a young lady—rather as Aramantha rambles through garden, meadows, wood, communes with birds, and runs into a man. Military imagery is common in both poems. Aramantha's tears over man's killing of the friendly cow suggests Marvell's "Nymph Complaining for the Death of her Faun"; and the detailed description of Aramantha's entry into a grove is close to Marvell's "Garden" and "Bermudas." The theme of the superiority of the pastoral, "natural" life appears also in Marvell's "Mower" poems.

Certain lyrics by both are merely contributions to conventional genres—the lady weeping, mourning, singing, or dancing; the pastoral-like dialogues; the country-house poems. The Alexis-Lucasta dialogue concludes with the lady's wish to fall into a perpetual sleep, "And oh! if night us undivided make,/Let us sleep still, and sleeping, never wake!" (261, 31–32); and Marvell's Thyrsis-Dorinda dialogue ends with the desire to pick poppies and, in never-ending sleep, to reach Elyzium, "So shall we smoothly pass away in sleep." The same Lovelace poem contains a line, "Love . . ./Creates alone fresh-bleeding bannerets," close to one in Marvell's "Unfortunate Lover," "This is the only Banneret/That ever Love created yet." The latter Marvell poem recalls in turn Lovelace's "Against the Love of Great Ones," which begins, "Unhappy youth, betrayed by faith." Lovelace's lady asks the low-born lover, "Wouldst thou with tempests lie? Then bow/To th' rougher furrows of her brow./Or make a thunderbolt thy choice?/ . . . Or 'gender with the lightning?" (282, 15–19); and Marvell's poem expands the image of storm at sea, "The Seas/Ruled and the Winds did what they please,/That my poor Lover floating lay . . ./Was cast away."

Marvell's most famous lyric, "To His Coy Mistress," was his contribution to the seduction-poem genre common in the seventeenth century. In its first stanza's graphic evocation of what might or should be, it approximates less the self-justifying, rationalizing assertions in poems like Lovelace's "The Scrutiny" or "Depose" than the dreaming fantasy of "Love Made in the First Age," and its remaining parts recall other Lovelace poems,

> Thus, although this marble must,
> As all things, crumble into dust,
> And though you find this fair-built tomb
> Ashes, as what lies in its womb.
>   (264, 37–40)

> What pity the whole world is but one ball.
>   (351, 18)

> Her fires, that with the sun kept race.
> (336, 27)

Lovelace's poem to Francis on the death of brother William has some parallels with Marvell's "Definition of Love": "Iron decrees of Destiny" (290, 15) suggests "Fate does Iron wedges drive" and "Iron gates of life." "One gallant thorough-made resolve/Doth starry influence dissolve" (19–20) is echoed by Marvell's "The Conjunction of the Mind,/And Opposition of the Stars."

Marvell's poem to Lovelace, as well as his "Tom May's Death," contains satiric attacks on the contemporary literary scene reminiscent of Lovelace's "On Sannazar." In the lines to Lovelace, Marvell contrasts the earlier (Caroline) age in which poets spoke well and with praise to the present (Commonwealth) in which

> He highest builds, who with most Art destroys,
> And against others Fame his owne employs.
>   The Ayre's already tainted with the swarms
> Of Insects which against you rise in arms.
> Word-peckers, Paper-rats, Book-scorpions,
> Of wit corrupted, the unfashion'd Sons;

so too Lovelace in his satire, after ironic advice on how today's poets may advance by attacking excellence, describes the overrunning of literature by the Vandals, Goths, "scorpions, . . . a mist of insects." In the May poem, Marvell brings in towering Jonson, "sworn enemy to all that do pretend." Ben angrily whips out Tom May, "Vandal, Goth,/Malignant Poet and Historian both" who has "prostituted . . . our spotless Knowledge and the Studies chaste"; and, in Lovelace's satire, all-judging Jonson is invoked to drive the money-changers and the women from the temple of poetry.[6]

The parallels with Milton are less clear but are of equal interest because of the marked difference in temperament of the two poets. When Milton echoes the Cavalier rhetoric, he does so in a negative way. The things the Cavalier yearns for, to "lie tangled in her hair" (284, 5), "Ev'ry tress . . . neatly tangled at the best" (248, 9–10), Milton entertains, "To sport with . . ./The tangles of Neaera's hair?" before abjuring. Several references in Lovelace to

plumbing the depths and ascending the heights—"And now what
heav'n must I invade, what sphere/Rifle" (346, 95–96), "dive to
the Abyss" (362, 97), "Interpret the deep mystery of all" (354,
108)—remind us not only of the actual subject and achievement
of *Paradise Lost* but also of the epic poet's early aspirations:
"Where the deep transported mind may soar/Above the wheeling
poles, and at Heaven's door/Look in."

The tableau in Lovelace's "Love Made in the First Age" of
golden lads and lasses living sensually without clothing yet without any sense of sin is Christianized by Milton in his scene of
Adam and Eve leading a happy life in prelapsarian Eden. Lovelace's "Naked as their own innocence" and "Each touch was naturally chaste" (329, 43, 41) recall the innocence of the first couple
("Then was not guilty shame") and their love-making, which Milton depicts as pure and holy sex. The special beds "softer than the
cygnet's down" are like Milton's bed of flower petals. Lovelace's
conjunction of nakedness and sinlessness, with the implied association of clothing and artifice, veiling, duplicity, recall Milton's attack on clothing: "[Adam and Eve were] eas'd the putting off/
These troublesome disguises which we wear."

Eve "her unadorned golden tresses wore,/Dishevell'd . . . in
wanton ringlets wav'd"; Aramantha walks with "loose hair" curled
by dew, sun, and wind, and is urged to dishevel her hair. Indeed,
the first half of Lovelace's pastoral, with its description of the heroine's idyllic life, is close to Book IV of *Paradise Lost*. The birds
usher in and out each day in epic and pastoral; Aramantha among
the flower of the garden,

> So like the Provence rose she walk'd,
> Flower'd with blush, with verdure stalk'd;
>
> . . . .
>
> Here her glad eye she largely feeds,
> And stands, 'mongst them, as they 'mong weeds;
> The flowers, in their best array,
>   (303, 35–36, 45–47)

is like Eve

> Veil'd in a Cloud of Fragrance, where she stood,
> Half spi'd, so thick the Roses blushing round

> About her glowed, oft stooping to support
> Each Flower of slender stalk.
>
> . . . .
>
> Herself, though fairest unsupported Flow'r.

Eve's Narcissus-like posture, soon after being created, of adoring her reflection in the pool and finally turning from that to the proper love of a man is also the subject of "Lucasta's Fan."

Several images and devices of rhetoric used by Lovelace were exploited with greater force by poets of the eighteenth and nineteenth centuries. The *zeugma* in "Love Made in the First Age"—"lads indifferently" cropping "a flower and a maidenhead," tippling "wine from the bunch, milk from the nipple," and squeezing "jellies" from "olive trees and bellies"—was refined by Pope in his "Rape of the Lock": "Files of . . . patches, Bibles, billets doux," "stain her honor or her new brocade . . . lose her heart, or necklace, at a ball." The compassionate, bemused observation of ant and grasshopper, followed by the universalizing of the creature's adverse experience, was perfected in Burns's "To a Mouse" and "To a Daisy." The celebration of wine, women, and song in "To Althea" and in "Loose Saraband [1659]" becomes central in Burns's poetry, notably "The Jolly Beggars."

Keats's nightingale ode juxtaposes immortal bird and mortal man even as "The Grasshopper" does insect and man, but Lovelace's man is able to endure the dark time which defeats the grasshopper: a case of mortal insect vis-à-vis relatively immortal man. The famous conclusion of the Urn ode, "Beauty is truth, truth beauty," is nebulously adumbrated by Lovelace's "For singing troth is but in tune to speak" (356, 6); even as is Byron's "music breathing from her face" by Lovelace's "music of her face"; and Shelley's "If winter comes, can spring be far behind?" by Lovelace's verbose,

> That mighty breath which blew foul Winter hither
> Can eas'ly puff it to a fairer weather.
> Why dost despair then, Frank? Aeolus has
> A Zephyrus as well as Boreas.
>
> (349, 51–54)

CHAPTER 10

Reputation and Achievement

I *Reputation*

LOVELACE'S reputation as a poet begins early indeed—in his twenty-first year. Though he had left Oxford two years earlier, his lines on the Princess Katherine were inserted into copies of a volume of elegies by Oxford students. Similarly, when Fletcher's *Wild Goose Chase* appeared in 1652, Lovelace's prefatory verses were printed in larger type than the others' and given the place of honor among them. He was evidently prominent in his time.

Another interesting sidelight is the recent discovery, amid sober entries for 1643–44 in an ordnance notebook, of doodles of the first stanza of "The Scrutiny." It is amusing to think of an ordnance officer or clerk passing the tedious hours by attempting to jot down the stanzas of a brash new poem by a fashionable young poet. Judging from the numerous reprintings this poem underwent in various collections during the rest of the century, "The Scrutiny" became one of Lovelace's most popular. But the best known of his poems was, of course, "To Althea," referred to as early as 1644–45 and continually reprinted.[1]

Before *Lucasta* came out in 1649, Marvell wrote introductory lines which, after decrying the decline in culture, spoke of "insects" who rose against Lovelace, partly because of his role in the Kentish Petition. The implication is that the volume had not yet been licensed but was being scrutinized in accordance with the Printing Ordinance. Politically innocuous as the poems seem to us, their publication may well have been delayed for a while.

The rest of Marvell's poem sketches a different sort of Lovelace fame—as a ladies' man. John Tatham makes similar remarks in his prefatory lines, which suggest that Lovelace also enjoyed repute as poet: the lasses, he says, in Lovelace's absence "do only sigh thy Airs," and the swains "deny to write a line/And do only talk of thine"; he urges Lovelace "by sweet Athea's voice" to return. This passage indicates that Lovelace was known around 1644 as the poet of Althea rather than of Lucasta and that the prison poem, the only one to Althea, was popular before the 1649 confinement and publication of the book. Praised by friends, Lovelace's poetry was set to music by such eminent composers of the day as Henry Lawes and John Wilson. In Cotgrave's *Wit's Interpreter* (1655), the leading mid-seventeenth-century anthology, one and a half of his poems appeared.

Though Lovelace received brief honorific mention in Joshua Poole's 1657 *English Parnassus*, in Edward Phillips's 1675 *Theatrum Poetarum*, and in William Winstanley's 1687 *Lives of the Most Famous English Poets*, his popularity during the next century and a half was not equal to that of Suckling, Randolph, Cartwright, Habington, Cleveland. Indeed his friend Suckling, in presenting a critique of major and minor contemporary poets, including himself, in "A Session of Poets," makes no mention of Lovelace.

A curious indication that Lovelace had, nevertheless, become the archetypal Cavalier very early was brought to light not too long ago. In his edition of Lovelace, C. H. Wilkinson, at the suggestion of G. Thorn-Drury, pointed out that in Sir Charles Sedley's Restoration play, *The Mulberry Garden*, there are—besides paraphrases of and allusions to famous Lovelace lyrics like "Wars," "Althea," "To Lucasta. From Prison"—numerous parallels with the poet's putative life: his loss of property to the wars and of his beloved to another man; his part in Royalist activities; his being arrested over an incriminating paper and as a by-product of the search for someone else; the unusual name Althea. The ending is happy in the play, as not in life; but, even so, a character's gallant surrender of the lady may perhaps be a picture of some similar action on Lovelace's part and thus give renewed life to Wood's story of Lucasta. If the identification is correct, Sedley's play is an interesting sign of how Lovelace's career and poetry captured the imagination of his age.

In the first half of the eighteenth century, the Neo-Classical Augustan period, Lovelace was not referred to anywhere. He seemed not to have existed at all. He reappeared on the poetic scene in 1765, or just a little over a hundred years after his death, with the publication of Thomas Percy's *Reliques of Ancient English Poetry*, which contained "Wars" and "Althea." The first attempt at a critical appreciation was made in *The Gentleman's Magazine* of 1791–92, over the pseudonym of Cliffordiensis, generally presumed to have been Sir Samuel Egerton Brydges. The period 1817–18 saw the publication, by S. W. Singer, of all of Lovelace's poems, but with expurgations and deletions. Both *Lucastas* came out in 1864 in one volume edited by W. Carew Hazlitt, who segregated the poems by topic. Thus in Part I (1649) all verses addressed to Lucasta (and Aramantha) were gathered, followed by the ones to Ellinda, and rounded off by miscellaneous works and commendatory poems. Hazlitt's notes were good, but his biographical material was superseded by A. E. Waite, who in 1884 brought new documents to light.

The many twentieth-century students of Donne's influence, emphasizing Lovelace's greater proximity to the Metaphysicals than to the "Sons of Ben," found him, vis-à-vis the master, sorely wanting. Amateur and gentleman, he seemed, though modeling his work on Donne's, to be working in a style uncongenial to him. Some of his best things, like "To . . . Sea," are most memorable when most Metaphysical, yet Lovelace remained on the fringes of the Donne tradition. A piece like "La Bella Bona Roba" is static next to Donne's not because of a lack of "wit" or ingenuity but because to Donne "wit" was a means of expressing complex states of mind and achieving intellectual self-mastery; to the Cavalier, "wit" was exercised and enjoyed for its own sake. The "Grasshopper" shows that he should have followed the simplicity and clarity of Horace rather than the abstruseness of Donne, but he was unable to approach Herrick's grace and too indifferent, too "witty" to move from Metaphysical to the rising Neo-Classical vein. His effort in preserving the courtly stance of polished detachment nevertheless foreshadowed the elegant social wit of the Augustans.[2]

The greatest year in Lovelace's posthumous fame, 1925, saw the publication of the definitive edition of his poems and of the only book-length study of his work. In a lavishly annotated and illustrated edition, bringing together all the biographical material, C. H. Wilkinson furnished the best account yet of the poet's life. Issued in a limited printing, the edition reappeared in one volume, shorn of its illustrations, in 1930; and it is not likely to be superseded for some time.

As a scholar who lived with Lovelace's work more than any

other person, Wilkinson also provided the lengthiest, most detailed and considered evaluation of it. Two or three of the poems, he notes, are everywhere anthologized and given a "high place among the lyrics of an age supreme in the art of song"; but they have overshadowed his other lyrics. Wilkinson is aware that this neglect is partly justified: one of the "mob of gentlemen who wrote with ease," Lovelace, following the Cavalier imitation of devices made fashionable by Donne, wrought "slender conceits and labored particularities." His many obvious faults—obscurity, discontinuity, frigidity, slovenliness, striving after effect, lack of the light touch—add up to a case of (as Douglas Bush later put it) "the pernicious anemia of the secular Metaphysical muse, with its dwindling from cosmic audacities into labored and eccentric artifice." Lovelace writes reams of dull verse, minor poems of a minor poet; and, despite incidental attractions, his superlative achievements remain a handful of poems. On the other hand, these successes are the product of an informed sense of art, not mere luck; and a considerable portion of his work is better than is generally believed. Though he sometimes carries a conceit off with the best of them, he does not, when most effective, depend on Metaphysical effects; he is not sufficiently profound or clever to take naturally to this mode of writing. At his best, he exhibits a grace and ease, spontaneity and elegance in the manner of Wyatt. Lovelace is, in short, a worthy representative of the Cavalier class of amateur poets; "he writes very well for a gentleman," but, as a reviewer put it, "he can write worse than any other poet in England who can write as well." [3]

The other event of 1925, C. H. Hartmann's book on Lovelace, proved disappointing. Utilizing a faded nineteenth-century approach, it assumed that every lyric is a "sincere" autobiographical expression and therefore usable as a document. Neither did this study, being limited in its survey of the culture of the age, have much new to say about the "Cavalier spirit." Hartmann's conclusions are predictable: Lovelace writes much that is fashionable, complimentary, occasional, trival, and only when inspired by love (Lucasta) and honor (Charles I) is he a real Cavalier and a fine poet.

Various reviews greeted the Wilkinson edition but none by a major critic or poet. The most stimulating, in the *Times Literary Supplement*, forwarded the thesis that Lovelace is, in such works as "Aramantha," not at all Cavalier but Elizabethan; that he has more in common with Wyatt, Surrey, Raleigh, and the "miniature grace" of Campion than with Suckling, Carew, and Stanley. So too, a generation later, David Daiches, relating the chivalric and Royalist ideal to Sidney, Raleigh, and the older Renaissance tradition of courtesy, associated Lovelace's poems, at their best, with the strengths of Wyatt. The anachronistic Neo-Platonic Sidneyan and Spenserian values of ideal love, beauty, honor were given one last expression by Lovelace. Mario Praz, on the other hand, found Lovelace, despite his slender contribution and derivativeness, not only of his time but the most picturesque and striking Caroline poet—an important index of seventeenth-century customs and predilections, of the complexity of the age's poetic development.[4]

Though we speak nowadays of Lovelace, Suckling, Carew in one breath, the earlier centuries did not. Often ignoring Lovelace, they lumped Carew with Suckling. The two indeed share a libertine strain, but it is found in Lovelace also. Moreover, neither Suckling nor Lovelace approaches Carew at his best; they share his urbanity, not his artistic devotion and consistency. To F. R. Leavis, Carew, as the bearer, with Marvell, of the line of wit from Jonson and Donne to Pope, deserves better than to be bracketed with Suckling and Lovelace.

The consensus of modern criticism regards Lovelace more unequal as an artist but also more serious at his best than Suckling. As craftsman, Lovelace is closer to Carew; but his art is not so rewarding because his grotesque ingenuity, beyond Carew's, defeats him. Of the three poets, Lovelace is sometimes the least naturally, at other times the most naturally, a Metaphysical poet. Possessed of a curious mind, he has a wider range of interests, themes, and images. But lacking Donne's erudition and insight, he points the way to the dead end of John Cleveland's artificial, contorted style in wandering beyond the limits set by his subject and by the capacity of words. He could sing as sweetly as Carew or Suckling, yet not be as polished as the one or as natural as the other. In an age of dilettantism, he was more uneven than they.

Some find Lovelace quite unlike Suckling or Carew. He uniquely has a rare strain of sensuousness and tenderness. He seems more of a dreamer than the other two, but he also observes nature more closely—whether recording the ubiquity of conflict in it or (in the pastoral) its repose and beauty. Above all, Lovelace expresses a sense of honor and chivalry that is alien to the others. Suckling and Carew dramatize the Cavalier's worldliness; Lovelace presents the Cavalier ideal. His gentility was so strong as to make his attempts at Sucklingesque cynicism seem to some unconvincing, as though he were trying to prove he was no prig. To Albert Baugh, he belongs rather with Godolphin and Montrose as the "noblest and most hapless of the Cavaliers," poets of slender performance but fragrant memory. In the two famous exalted lyrics, Lovelace, expressing the "sense of honor in manly alliance with his love," is, therefore, *the* exemplary Cavalier spirit.[5]

The postwar years produced several essays with fresh insights. In *Velvet Studies*, C. V. Wedgwood speaks (like an earlier reviewer) of the anachronistic, escapist aspect of Lovelace. She stresses a certain self-mockery; many a conceit of his is a piece of bravura, of deliberate showing off, as though the poet were to turn to us admiringly and say, "Now isn't that a quaint conceit I've got!" Lovelace deliberately marries the sublime to the ridiculous in order to raise a smile. Geoffrey Walton in "The Cavalier Poets," finds Lovelace a courtier and soldier of European culture expressing with clarity and sophistication "the surviving code of chivalry and the public values of the seventeenth-century country gentleman" and, in the insect poems, the "private interests of the Kentish squire and the rural roots of the Cavalier." Not a "Son of Ben," Lovelace lacked the discipline that would have controlled somewhat "the suns and flowers that burst forth a little too brightly in this poetry."

Robin Skelton notes, in his *Cavalier Poets*, a contrast in Lovelace's work between the polite, social, formal poetry and the celebration of food, wine, music, women; between the pretentious, ornate compliments and the insect fables, the charming drink and prison poems. Even the latter kind, though vigorous, passionate, and conversational, do not put us into familiar relationship with the speaker, do not convey a presence. Without emotional involvement, the poet seems to be playing with words and ideas, enjoying his virtuosity and providing "well-mannered and graceful diversion for the cultured reader." His wit has an impersonal withdrawn air that is unlike the animal spirits of Carew and Suckling in pursuit of women. Not a questioning soul, Lovelace accepts at face value fashionable compliment, cosmic similitude, pastoral language. He presents moral sentiments in lucid lines of restrained rhythm reinforced with parallelism, antithesis, paradox. This "poetry of ceremony rather than spontaneity" furnishes, adds Skelton, a "sense of inner dignity of humanity . . . lacking in Carew and Suckling." Lovelace's lines have a sweetness, even his humor has more gentleness than raillery; without genius, he has his own radiance. His Cavalier poems are, however, his least typical; the strength, control, gaiety, courage, personal touch of "To Althea" are rare.

The latest essay, one of the best, is by Bruce King. Stimulating, even if wrong-headed, it logically extends random suggestions of earlier writers and constructs a portrait of Lovelace as a modern *Angst*-ridden Existentialist. King begins with the assertion, first made by Empson and Holland, that Lovelace's famous two "Cavalier" poems really are about the flight from the demands of love and the beloved—an analysis resting on the assumption that what the poems say literally is not what they mean. King's approach was anticipated as well by Walton's remark that Lovelace, though not often vulgar like Suckling, exhibits a surprising vein of deeper cynicism; by Skelton's contrast between the animal spirits of Carew and Suckling and the withdrawn air of Lovelace; by Alvarez' complaint at Lovelace's posturing.[6]

King finds the image of Lovelace as a gay, debonair Cavalier spirit mainly Restoration and Victorian propaganda. Most readers, who have missed the deep streak of skepticism and cynicism in Lovelace, accept the affirmative poems at face value instead of seeing them for what they are: examples of a disillusioned mind desperately trying to hang on to anything in the world. Exploiting venerable ideals, the poems are not affirmations of the chivalric code but a turning inwards. The ideals celebrated are mere postures, defensive masks—psychological necessities to ward off reality. Lovelace's confidence continually falters, for demoralization lies behind the affirmation.

The cynicism is not merely political but affects his whole sensibility, as is seen from the way references to prison appear in all sorts of unlikely places. Not only defeat in war but a complete spiritual and physical insecurity is intimated by "Advice"; all activity, on land as well as on sea, leads to disaster, as do even inactivity and the "golden mean." "The Grasshopper" gives a medieval picture of mutability in all things and dismisses conviviality as an external crutch that is doomed like the insect.

Without the values arbitrarily and blindly imposed on a disintegrating society, Lovelace's sentiments turn coarse. The lesser poems are more completely disillusioned and offer only the crudest sort of protection or none at all. In the "Loose Saraband [1659]" the carefree Cavalier attitude suddenly appears a desperate reaction to brutal reality, and the withdrawal into drink and gross sensuality is made in a manner more aggressive than that found in other libertine poets. Lovelace's libertinism, lacking the balance of Carew's, suggests a total disillusionment with experience; it stems from hatred of life rather than love of the senses. The 1659 volume, especially, seems to King distrustful, violent, paranoiac in its reaction to society. It fills the natural world with emblems of distasteful reality—ant, fly, snail. The law of animal life is the law of man; life itself is insecure and empty. With such an interpretation, Lovelace may be truly said to have been made currently relevant.

II *Achievement*

In arriving at a final evaluation of Lovelace's poetry, we cannot ignore his limitations. His tastes are simple; his mind bare of complex ideas. His unquestioning commitments to lady and king are childlike and, though intensely asserted, of but passing interest. He has no theory of politics, love, or indeed anything. Unless it be the epicurean flourish in the face of a lowering night, he has no central vision, no abiding emotion. The Cavalier posture for which he is so well known is but a glimmer in a few poems. The courtly amatory, like the drinking and cynical seduction poems, are sometimes amusing but heavily derivative. The insect and creature poems are peculiar to him and affecting in a limited way. He is not haunted by time, death, or history; by loss of prosperity or rise of Cromwell; by *carpe diem* thoughts. Nor is he moved to towering rejection or acceptance of love or regicide. Except for the problems of liberty and confinement and of the conflict in nature, which are at the heart of his best things, many great themes and issues pass by him—despite his living through a dramatic epoch.

It is undeniable that Lovelace wrote numerous poems which

remain, after all explication, bad; that even his good poems are often static and two-dimensional; that his style is marred by all the things earlier critics listed; that he is, in short, a minor poet. Yet, in spite of all, Lovelace's successes, as this study has attempted to show, have *not* been limited to the two well-known poems. His work contains a substantial number of beautiful lines and images, most of which we have examined.

He evinces virtuosity in several kinds of poetry. We saw that in the Carolingian period octosyllabic verse became the vogue. While Lovelace offers no poem of quality comparable to Marvell's "Coy Mistress" or Milton's twin poems, he manages quite a few successful couplets. Many of the good, limpid octosyllabics are in his pastoral. Some of them have satiric thrust to them; and indeed, the satiric pentameter couplet, is also an area of the poet's proficiency too little noticed. Another forte of Lovelace's is his conclusion. Though incapable of the Miltonic resolution—for lack of supreme mastery in the body of the poem—he yet can achieve fine lines at the end of stanza or lyric.

Besides the stereotyped image of Lovelace the Cavalier, we have seen the cynical seducer as well as the wailing, unrequited lover; the biting satirist of the social scene, alongside the bemused observer of insects; the celebrator of the arts no less than the man haunted by conflict and prison; the recorder of small incidents and of a great dilemma. The important Lovelace themes are: in the microcosmic life of insects and small beasts, combat and entrapment; in the dissolving social structure, imprisonment; in amatory matters, separation. These adversities can be overcome by a renewed dedication to transcendent lover and honor, or by Epicurean conviviality and retirement, or by hedonistic abandonment to drink and sex.

In the insect poems, confinement, unrelieved by spiritual self-mastery, means ignominious, painful death. For man, on the other hand, blessed or cursed with consciousness, incarceration can be redoubled because, "grief too can manacle the mind" and physical constraint may not be so severe as the emotional subjection to the lady. But that same human consciousness provides liberation: in one poem, through wine, song, and self-abandonment; in another, through honor, by renewal of allegiance to the king amidst general dissolution. In "To Althea" and "The Guiltless Lady," physical confinement is transcended by love, wine, the certainty of one's

own integrity, or by one's personal magnetism. In "The Scrutiny"
and in "Wars," the confinement is entirely spriritual, stemming
from possession by woman, love; freedom is found by turning to
other sexual liaisons, or by renewed devotion to the ideal of
honor.

In the last analysis, the haunting sense of universal conflict and
entrapment, and the problem of liberty and confinement, are part
of his one recurring motif or major theme—"Honor." He is of two
minds about honor: giving himself with equal zest to deriding it in
drink or erotic lyric or to lauding it, with reference to king or lady,
in poems on prison, camp, or court. Whether writing of mute insect or Renaissance gentleman, Lovelace has sketched the range
of responses to the universal predicament of confinement—from
passive death to active choice of pleasure or something "higher."
His basic contribution to English literature, therefore, is his dramatization of the two ways of acting in the face of disaster—by
self-abandonment or by self-discipline; or, as a moral relativist
might describe it, by two different modes of self-abandonment.

Evaluating his total output, we can say that Lovelace is least
inspired in his occasional and Petrarchan love poetry, better in his
jaunty erotica and sociopolitical stuff, best at the juncture of
courtly, amatory, and political which he made peculiarly his own
area. His insect poems likewise constitute a contribution to the
age. Hardly anything of his poetry is original; but the same can be
said of Shakespeare, and not originality but aptness in expressing
what oft was thought is the criterion. Lovelace manages to give
genre pieces like "The Grasshopper" or "The Fair Beggar" a touch
of his own. The existence of twin poems on the same subjects—on
the snail, the fly caught, the patch on the lady's face, Lucasta at
the bath, himself in prison, Lely's painting—suggests a tentative-
ness on the part of the poet or, more likely, a certain open-
mindedness: a willingness to experiment, to re-examine appear-
ances from varying perspectives.

But—besides individual lines, images, octosyllabics, conclusions, satiric couplets; besides beautiful fragments from flawed
poems like "Aramantha" and "On Sannazar"; besides a recurring
theme or two—does Lovelace present more substantial, complete
achievement; any self-contained, finished works of art, however
brief, any "well-wrought sonnets"?

From his collection of a hundred and three poems we can sal-

vage about forty, or two-fifths. While this may not be a high per-
centage compared with Donne, Herbert, Marvell, it is substantial.
Of these forty, some fifteen to twenty are effective and readable;
repay study; change our view of life ever so little; leave us wiser,
amused, or moved. Each has its flaws, to be sure, but none is
incapacitated by them. This list of poems certainly would include
"A Paradox," "Gratiana singing and dancing," "To Ellinda . . .
written," "The Vintage to the Dungeon," "A Guiltless Lady,"
"The Apostacy," "La Bella Bona Roba," "In Allusion," "The Duel,"
"Dialogue. Lute and Voice," "An Anniversary," "Painture," "Valiant Love," "A Fly . . . Cobweb," "To Lucasta. From Prison,"
"You Are Deceived," "The Advice."

There are, moreover, a dozen poems which are very good; in
these the flaws are nearly effaced by striking images or lines, by
effective rhetoric, or by a sense of humor. This group, containing
no masterpieces, is typical of that great age of lyric poetry when
so many men were able to write beautiful poems with little apparent effort. It includes "To . . . Hair," "Depose," "The Rose,"
"The Scrutiny," "Loose Saraband [1659]," "Cupid Far Gone,"
"The Ant," "On Sannazar," "The Snail," "A Fly . . . Claret,"
"Love . . . First Age," "Strive Not." And there are the half-dozen
perfect poems, the masterpieces from Lovelace's pen which take
their place with the finer lyrics of the age and which are in all the
anthologies: "To . . . Sea," "To . . . Wars," "The Grasshopper,"
"Ellinda's Glove," "To Althea," "The Fair Beggar." Of these, "Ellinda's Glove" and "The Fair Beggar" have hardly been noticed
until lately; "To . . . Sea" and "The Grasshopper" have been
coming into prominence in the twentieth century; and, of course,
"To . . . Wars" and "To Althea" have been acknowledged for the
last two hundred years as supreme utterances of the heroic temperament in duress; as the swan song of the old order seen in its
noblest moment; as, in Grierson's famous words, the "only poems
which suggest what 'Cavalier' came to mean when glorified by
defeat." [7]

What is Lovelace's place in seventeenth-century English literature? If we put Shakespeare and Milton in the first rank, the peers
of other world geniuses; Donne, Jonson, Herbert, Marvell, Dryden in the second rank of consistently very fine to excellent poets;
Vaughan, Crashaw, Carew, Herrick in the third rank, of good to
very good talents; then Lovelace no doubt belongs with Suckling,

Lord Herbert, Cowley, Waller in a fourth category of sporadically good poets who are certainly superior to Stanley, Denham, Habington, Traherne. Fourth class does not sound very exalted, but it is no mean achievement to be accounted among the leading dozen poets in a century of very great poetry.

Notes and References

Chapter One

1. This sketch of Lovelace's life is based on three authorities: A. E. Waite, "Lovelace," *The Gentleman's Magazine*, CCLVII (1884), 459–475; C. H. Hartmann, *The Cavalier Spirit* (London, 1925), pp. 1–125; C. H. Wilkinson, ed., *The Poems of Lovelace* (Oxford, 1930), pp. xiii–lviii, 9–11, 223, 231, 233, 249, 260, 325–27, 345. Occasionally useful is Philip Lindsay, *For King or Parliament* (London, 1949), pp. 170–202. The earliest sources of information are the somewhat unreliable pair, John Aubrey (*Brief Lives*, ed. O. L. Dick [Ann Arbor, 1957], p. 192) and Anthony à Wood (*Athenae Oxoniensis*, ed. P. Bliss [London, 1817], III, 460–63). The latter is more detailed. Sir Egerton Brydges shed some light in 1791 (*The Gentleman's Magazine*, LXI, ii, 1094–95; LXII, i, 99, 135, 166–67, 320–21; ii, 604–5, 971–72), as did W. Carew Hazlitt in his 1864 edition of the poems. Wilkinson's is the most authoritative essay.

2. Anthony à Wood, p. 460.

3. The best evocations of Lovelace's milieu at court are J. B. Fletcher, "*Précieuses* at the Court of Charles I," *Journal of Comparative Literature*, I (1903), 120–53; Margaret Pickel, *Charles I as Patron of Poetry and Drama* (London, 1936), esp. pp. 15, 17–25, 40, 69–95, 125–27, 157–71; C. V. Wedgwood, "Cavalier Poetry and Cavalier Politics," *Velvet Studies* (London, 1946), pp. 15–32. A recently discovered fact is discussed by Herbert Berry and E. K. Timings, "Lovelace at Court," *Modern Language Notes*, LXIX (1954), 396–98. For a contemporary definition of the Cavalier ideal, see Herrick's "His Cavalier."

4. Waite, p. 464.

5. Hartmann, p. 47.

6. Waite, p. 466; Wood, p. 462; Wilkinson, p. xlii.

7. Aubrey, p. 192; Lindsay, p. 177; Hartmann, p. 77.

8. Waite, p. 472.

9. Wood, p. 462–63; Waite, p. 475; Wilkinson, p. liii.

10. Lindsay, p. 202.

11. Wood, p. 462; all quotations of Lovelace's poetry are taken

from *Minor Poets of the Seventeenth Century*, ed. R. G. Howarth (London, 1931).

12. Waite, p. 474; Hartmann, pp. 72–76.

Chapter Two

1. On the theme of music and poetry, see John Hollander, *The Untuning of the Sky* (Princeton, 1961), pp. 368–74.

2. On the theme of painting and poetry, see Jean Hagstrum, *The Sister Arts* (Chicago, 1958), pp. 109, 122–23, 178, 224. With reference to the line, "Thou sorrow canst design without a tear," see the thesis of Bernard Berenson's *Piero della Francesca*.

3. This genre exists as early as the *Greek Anthology*, whose poem V, 163, is about a bee attracted to the lady's skin. In Guarini (Madrigal xxxvii) it is a butterfly; in Carew, a fly; in Cartwright, a gnat. Cf. also Jonson's "Hour Glass," Cleveland's "Upon a Fly" and "Fuscura, or the Bee."

4. The influence of Dutch still-life painting on Lovelace's insect and small-beast poems was first suggested by Mario Praz, in rev. of Wilkinson's edition, *Modern Language Review*, XXI (1926), 322, and can be verified by a glance at the plates, in Ingvar Bergström, *Dutch Still Life Painting in the Seventeenth Century*, trans. C. Hedström and Gerald Taylor (London, 1956), of paintings by Ambrosius Bosschaert the Elder and the Younger, Georg Hofnagel, Jacques de Gheyn, Balthasar van der Ast.

5. The combat of these two birds is the subject of a 1590 emblem by Joachim Camerarius and a French poem by Claude Gauchet; the description of the funeral is in the manner of the bird elegies of Ovid and Statius; see on this, Kitty Scoulay, *Natural Magic* (Oxford, 1965), pp. 74–81, 99–103.

6. Geoffrey Walton, *Metaphysical to Augustan* (London, 1955), p. 36; for other pertinent observations, see Robin Skelton, *Cavalier Poets* (London, 1960), p. 31; A. Lytton Sells, *Animal Poetry* (London, 1955), pp. 61, 95, 104–8, 110, 175, 293; K. E. McEuen, *Classical Influences Upon the Tribe of Ben* (Cedar Rapids, 1939), pp. 35–38.

7. Hugh Kenner, ed., *Seventeenth Century Poetry* (New York, 1964), p. 371; Scoulay, p. 103; Skelton, p. 31.

8. Bruce King, "Green Ice and a Breast of Proof," *CE*, XXVI (1964), 511–15.

Chapter Three

1. For the translation from Sarbiewski, see J. C. Arens, "Sarbiewski's Ode Against Tears," *Neophilologus*, XLVII (1963), 236–39.

2. Maren-Sofie Røstvig, *The Happy Man* (Oslo, 1954), pp. 46–48, 50, 53–54, 60–61, 72, 76, 174, 187.

3. McEuen, pp. 108–10; see especially Horace, *Odes* II, x.

4. The pleasures of the country retreat, a common subject of poetry and prose, were often celebrated in seventeenth-century France and even more, amid the Civil War, in England. Especially close here are two poems written a decade later by a far greater poet on the opposite side in the political struggle—Milton's sonnets XX and XXI. Lovelace's original contribution to this genre was to fuse it with the grasshopper poems. Many such lyrics of singing or drinking locusts, cicada, grasshoppers are to be found in the *Greek Anthology*, principally in VII, 189–201. The Horatian poems to which Lovelace is indebted are *Epodes* ix, xiii, and *Odes* I, ix; II, ii, iii; III, xvii; IV, xii. See also Ausonius, III, iii, 10ff. For a fuller analysis of this poem and its background, see D. C. Allen, who, in *Seventeenth-Century English Poetry*, ed. W. R. Keast (Oxford, 1962), pp. 280–89, emphasizes the Christian overtones. For the biblical sidelight, see Joan Grundy, "Marvell's Grasshoppers," *Notes and Queries*, CCII (1957), p. 142. Røstvig (p. 469) detects the influence here of the Christian Stoicism of Sarbiewski (*Odes*, IV, xxiii, "Ad Cicadam"), while McEuen (p. 10) thinks this piece of Epicurean reflectiveness is Lovelace's only real approach to writing a Classical ode. Bruce King (pp. 514–15) finds not Christianity, Stoicism, or Epicureanism but pessimism; he stresses also the implied political contrast between the thrifty Puritan-like ant and the singing aristocratic grasshopper. See also H. G. Wright, "The Theme of Solitude and Retirement," *Études Anglaises*, VII (1954), 22; Scoulay, pp. 108–12.

5. See Wilkinson, pp. lvi ff., and E. E. Duncan-Jones, "Two Allusions in Lovelace's poems," *Modern Language Review*, LI (1956), 407–8.

6. See Willa Evans, "Lovelace's Concept of Prison Life," *Philological Quarterly*, XXVI (1947), 62–68.

7. Whether "gods" (7) should be "birds" is the subject of controversy: see Wilkinson's notes; Margoliouth, rev. of Wilkinson's ed., *Review of English Studies*, III (1927), 90; A. C. Judson, "A Forgotten Lovelace MS," *Modern Language Notes*, XXXVII (1922), 407–410; Grierson, quoted in Wilkinson. To all this we might add the observation that "angels" (Christian) could supersede "gods" (pagan) and that "gods" is made necessary by "Love" (Cupid) in line one. See also C. V. Wedgwood, *Poetry and Politics Under the Stuarts* (Cambridge, 1960), pp. 106–8.

8. See Wedgwood, *Politics*, p. 192; William Empson, *Seven Types of Ambiguity* (New York, 2nd ed., 1947), pp. 209–11; Norman Holland, p. 52, n. 8.

9. For contemporary French expressions of the thought by Voiture and Pellisson-Fontanier, see Praz, p. 320 and Hartmann, pp. 45–46.

10. Hartmann, pp. 45–46; E. Wyndham Hulme, "Lovelace's Song to Althea," *Notes and Queries,* CXCV (1950), p. 98.

Chapter Four

1. L. C. Knights, "On the Social Background of Metaphysical Poetry," *Scrutiny,* XIII (1945), 37–52; see also Robin Skelton, *Cavalier Poets* (London, 1960), pp. 10, 14, 28, 43; Wedgwood, *Politics,* pp. 30–33, 203–4; Felix Schelling, *The English Lyric* (New York, 1913), pp. 91–92. This genre derives from the country-retreat poems of Horace and Martial; Rhodes Dunlap, in *Works of Carew* (Oxford, 1949), pp. 225, 256, sees Martial III, lviii, as the prototypic country-house poem, whereas Røstvig (p. 82) nominates X, xlvii, to which we might add XII, xviii.

2. *New York Review of Books,* November 9, 1967, p. 6.

3. On the Kentish Petition, see Margoliouth, pp. 89–95; on the "Public Faith" see Wedgwood, *Politics,* pp. 83, 108, 111. For widely differing dissents, see M. M. Ross, in *Poetry and Dogma* (New Brunswick, 1954), pp. 131–32, and King, pp. 512–13. •

4. See Wedgwood, *Politics,* pp. 73–74, 87, 191; Willa Evans, "Lovelace's 'Mock Song,'" *Philological Quarterly,* XXIV (1945), 317–328; E. F. Hart, "The Answer Poem of the Early Seventeenth Century," *Review of English Studies* (1956), pp. 19–20.

5. For other comments on this poem, see McEuen, pp. 51, 60–61; J. B. Emperor, p. 90; Duncan-Jones, pp. 407–9.

Chapter Five

1. Gosse, in *The English Poets,* ed. T. H. Ward (New York, 1908), II, 181; Williamson, *The Donne Tradition* (Cambridge, 1930), p. 208; A. C. Baugh, *A Literary History of England* (New York, 1948), p. 660; Walton in *From Donne to Marvell,* ed. B. Ford (London, 1956), p. 171).

2. Elton, *The English Muse* (London, 1933), p. 229; Grierson and Bullough, *The Oxford Book of Seventeenth-Century Verse* (Oxford, 1934), p. viii; Bush, *English Literature in the Earlier Seventeenth Century* (Oxford, 2nd ed., 1962), p. 123; Hollander, pp. 342–44, 394; Walton in *From Donne,* p. 171; Bald, *Donne's Influence in English Literature* (Gloucester, Mass., 1932), p. 20; Reeves, *A Short History of English Poetry* (New York, 1962), p. 97.

3. Wedgwood, *Politics,* p. 3; cf. Williamson, p. 209; Miles, *The Continuity of Poetic Language* (Los Angeles, 1951), pp. 53–54.

4. Mark Van Doren, *Introduction to Poetry* (New York, 1951), pp. 21–26.

5. Norman Holland, "Literary Value: A Psychoanalytic Approach," *Literature and Psychology,* XIV (1964), 43–55.

6. G. F. Jones, "Lov'd I Not Honour More: The Durability of a Literary Motif," *Comparative Literature*, XI (1959), 131–43.

7. N. H. Pearson, "Lovelace's 'To . . . Wars,'" *Explicator* (1949), VII, 8, #58; H. M. Richmond, "Response to Holland," *Literature and Psychology*, XIV (1964), 116–27.

8. This observation is made by Richmond and Holland. Lovelace borrowed his famous line from William Habington's "In the chaste Nunn'ry of her breasts," as was first noted by B. Wendell, *The Temper of the Seventeenth Century* (New York, 1904), p. 140, and Gosse, p. 182. For other comments on the poem see Skelton, p. 27; Bush, p. 122; David Daiches, *A Critical History of English Literature* (New York, 1960), I, 382; L. B. Salomon, *The Rebellious Lover* (Philadelphia, 1931), p. 145; H. M. Richmond, *The School of Love* (Princeton, 1964), pp. 152, 315; Bruce King, p. 512; John Ciardi, *How Does a Poem Mean?* (Boston, 1959), pp. 929–32. In "Lovelace's 'Flie,'" *Notes and Queries* (1955), pp. 428–29, N. Nathan argues that "flie," the original spelling in line 4, means "flee" rather than "fly." The shift from informal "thy" (3) to formal "you" (10) and back to informal "thee" (11) parallels the rich change from "sweet" to "dear."

Chapter Six

1. This song was one of Lovelace's most popular. See Wilkinson, Letter to *Times Literary Supplement*, August 14, 1937, pp. 592; Berry and Timings, p. 397. For analysis and comments, see Holland, pp. 43–55, 117–27; *Retrospective Review* (1821), p. 125; Walton in Ford, p. 171; Emperor, p. 16; Alvarez, p. 69; *Times Literary Supplement*, January 21, 1926, p. 41.

2. M. J. O'Regan, "The Fair Beggar," *Modern Language Review*, LV (1960), 186–99. This paper supersedes Pierre Legouis's "Deux thèmes," *Revue de littérature comparée*, V (1925), 139–51. See also McEuen, p. 133.

3. See Willa Evans, "To Amathea," *Philological Quarterly*, XXIII (1944), 129–34, and "An Early Lovelace Text," *Publications of the Modern Language Association*, LX (1945), 382–85, for curious theories.

4. Discussions of the golden age and libertinism are to be found in Louis Bredvold, "The Naturalism of Donne," *Journal of English and Germanic Philology*, XXII (1923), 471–502; Frank Kermode, *English Pastoral Poetry* (New York, 1952), pp. 25, 81–83, 241, 251, and "The Argument of Marvell's Garden," in Keast, pp. 292–95; Harry Levin, "Golden Age and the Renaissance," *Literary Views*, ed. C. C. Camden (Chicago, 1964), pp. 1–14; F. O. Henderson, "Traditions of *Précieux* and Libertine Poetry," *English Literary History*, IV (1937), 274–96; see also Mario Praz, "Stanley, Sherburne, Ayres," *Modern*

Language Review, XX (1925–26), 280–94, 419–31; McEuen, pp. 137, 191.

5. Compare Baudelaire's poem, "J'aime le souvenir de ces époques nues," for interesting changes in outlook caused by the circumstances and the era of the poet. While the Romans looked to the golden age as a time when the relations between men and women had not yet become mercenary (alluded to by Lovelace's "all-damning gold"), and while Lovelace emphasized in the golden age the innocence of such relations, untouched by the inhibitions and prohibitions of Christianity, Baudelaire, writing in an era when the blight of the Industrial Revolution was everywhere noticeable on the stunted bodies of working men, turns to the golden age as a period when men looked like people whose torsos were being used as they were meant to be by nature—"Exerçaient la santé de leur noble machine." ("I love the thought of those old naked days . . . Exercising the health of their noble machines.")

Chapter Seven

1. See Marius Bewley, *Scrutiny,* XVI (1949), 12–14; Alvarez, pp. 72–73.

Chapter Eight

1. G. N. Shuster, *The English Ode* (New York, 1940), pp. 90–91; Robert Shafer, *The English Ode* (Princeton, 1918), pp. 120–21; Carol Maddison, *Apollo and the Nine* (London, 1960), p. 305; McEuen, p. 110; Willa Evans, "The Rose," *Modern Language Quarterly,* VII (1946), 272–73.

2. This chart is based on the one hundred and three poems printed in the two volumes as Lovelace's and does not include the translations, which are almost entirely in couplets, and the "Voiture," not printed in either volume; the numbers in parentheses in line two refer to the three free-form poems mentioned above.

3. Duncan-Jones, pp. 407–8.

4. Wilkinson, p. lxxii; Willa Evans in *Publications of the Modern Language Association,* LX (1945), 382–85; *Philological Quarterly,* XXIV (1945), 317; *Modern Language Quarterly,* VII (1946), 273.

Chapter Nine

1. Skelton, pp. 9, 32, 43; for other definitions of and observations on Cavalier poetry, see R. G. Cox and Geoffrey Walton in *From Donne to Marvell,* pp. 61, 160–63, 168; R. A. Blanshard, "Carew and the Cavaliers," *Transactions of the Wisconsin Academy of Science, Arts, and Letters,* XLIII (1954), 97–101; Alvarez, p. 70; Wedgwood, *Velvet Studies,* pp. 15–32.

2. J. B. Emperor, *The Catullian Influence in English Poetry* (Columbia, Mo., 1928), p. 90.

3. For Classical influences, see McEuen, pp. 35–38, 108–10, 133, 144, 160–61, 178–79, 187, 215–16, 222–28, 270, 280, 283, 288, 290. For Continental Renaissance influences, see Praz, *Modern Language Review*, XX, 280–94, 419–31; XXI, 319–22.

4. Alvarez, p. 70.

5. C. F. Williamson, "Two Notes on . . . Lovelace," *Modern Language Review*, LII (1957), 229.

6. On the relations of Marvell and Lovelace, see Wilkinson's edition, p. 249; Wedgwood, *Seventeenth Century*, p. 117; Lindsay, p. 198; and, especially, L. N. Wall, "Some Notes on Marvell's Sources," *Notes and Queries*, CCII (1957), 70–73. Some of the parallels listed above were first noted by Wall and by Røstvig, pp. 248–49.

Chapter Ten

1. Wilkinson, pp. lxii ff., 260; Berry and Timings, pp. 396–98.

2. George Williamson, *The Donne Tradition* (Cambridge, Mass., 1930), pp. 208–9; R. C. Bald, *Donne's Influence in English Literature* (Gloucester, Mass., 1932), p. 20; R. L. Sharp, *From Donne to Dryden* (Chapel Hill, 1940), pp. 106–8; Alvarez, p. 73.

3. Wilkinson, pp. lxvi–lxxi; Bush, p. 123; *Times Literary Supplement*, January 21, 1926, p. 41.

4. Hartmann, pp. 116–19; Daiches, I, 382; Praz, 319–22.

5. The last few paragraphs are an amalgam of observations by the following: Blanshard, pp. 97–105; Thomas Seccombe in *Dictionary of National Biography* (1937–38), XII, 171; Bush, pp. 122–23; Baugh, pp. 660–61; Legouis and Cazamian, *A History of English Literature* (New York, rev. ed., 1935), p. 563; F. R. Leavis, *Revaluations* (New York, 1947), pp. 15, 37; H. Kenner, p. 371; Lindsay, p. 178.

6. C. V. Wedgwood, *Velvet Studies*, pp. 23, 27–28; *Seventeenth-Century Literature*, p. 72; Walton in *From Donne*, pp. 169–72; Skelton, pp. 26–34; Bruce King, "Green Ice and a Breast of Proof," *College English*, XXVI (1964), 511–15; Empson, p. 210; Holland, pp. 43–45; Alvarez, pp. 72–73.

7. Grierson, p. viii.

Selected Bibliography

PRIMARY SOURCES

LOVELACE, RICHARD. *Lucasta*. London: Thomas Harper, 1649.
————. *Lucasta: Posthume Poems*. Ed. Dudley Posthumus Lovelace and Eldred Revett. London: William Godbid, 1659.
————. *Works* in *Minor Poets of the Seventeenth Century*. Ed. R. G. Howarth. New York: E. P. Dutton & Co., 1931.

SECONDARY SOURCES

ALLEN, DON CAMERON. "Lovelace: The Grasshopper." *Seventeenth Century English Poetry*. Ed. W. R. Keast. New York: Oxford University Press, 1962. Learned analysis of the Classical and medieval background of the grasshopper, poem and symbol.
EVANS, WILLA M. "'Lawes' and Lovelace's 'Loose Saraband.'" *Publications of the Modern Language Association*, LIV (1939), 764–67.
————. "To Amathea." *Philological Quarterly*, XXIII (1944), 129–34.
————. "Lovelace's 'Mock Song.'" *Philological Quarterly*, XXIV (1945), 317–28.
————. "An Early Lovelace Text." *Publications of the Modern Language Association*, LX (1945), 382–85.
————. "'The Rose': A Song by Wilson and Lovelace." *Modern Language Quarterly*, VII (1946), 269–78.
————. "Lovelace's Concept of Prison Life in 'The Vintage to the Dungeon.'" *Philological Quarterly*, XXVI (1947), 62–68.
————. "Tormenting Fires." *Modern Language Quarterly*, IX (1948), 11–16.
A series of brief studies by an expert on the manuscripts of the period. Despite a propensity for assigning anonymous lyrics to Lovelace on tenuous grounds, Evans is good on the "Loose Saraband," "Mock Song," "Rose," "Vintage."
FLETCHER, J. B. "*Précieuses* at the Court of Charles I." *Journal of Comparative Literature*, I (1903), 120–53. Background material for the genteel aspect of Lovelace's poetry.
HARTMANN, CYRIL H. *The Cavalier Spirit and Its Influence on the Life and Work of Richard Lovelace*. London: G. Routledge & Sons, 1925. Adds nothing to the documentation of Waite and Wilkin-

son and only a little to the understanding of the "Cavalier Spirit" or of the poetry.

HENDERSON, F. O. "Traditions of *Précieux* and *Libertin* in Suckling's Poetry." *English Literary History,* IV (1937), 274–96. Background material for the libertine and French aspects of Lovelace's poetry.

HOLLAND, NORMAN. "Literary Value: A Psychoanalytic Approach." *Literature and Psychology,* XIV (1964), 43–55, 116–27. Excellent analysis of "The Scrutiny" and "To . . . Wars."

JONES, G. F. "Lov'd I Not Honour More: The Durability of a Literary Motif." *Comparative Literature,* XI (1959), 131–43. Thorough examination of the meaning of "honor" in earlier Western literature, as background material to "To . . . Wars."

KING, BRUCE. "Green Ice and a Breast of Proof." *College English,* XXVI (1964), 511–15. Stimulating if somewhat wrong-headed survey of Lovelace's *Weltanschauung* which turns him into a despairing, *Angst*-ridden modern.

O'REGAN, M. J. "The Fair Beggar—Decline of a Baroque Theme." *Modern Language Review,* IV (1960), 186–99. Scholarly and critical tracing of the various earlier, continental versions of the poem.

PEARSON, N. H. "Lovelace's 'To Lucasta . . . Wars.' " *Explicator,* VII (1949), 8, item 58. Fine brief explication of the poem.

PRAZ, MARIO. Review of Wilkinson's 1925 edition. *Modern Language Review,* XXI (1926), 319–22. Evaluation by a scholar acquainted with the continental background to seventeenth-century currents.

Review of Wilkinson's edition. *Times Literary Supplement,* January 21, 1926, p. 41. Presents Lovelace as a belated, misplaced Elizabethan in a time out of joint.

SKELTON, ROBIN. *The Cavalier Poets.* "Writers and their Work," No. 117. London: Longmans, Green, 1960. Sympathetic appreciation of Lovelace's strengths.

VAN DOREN, MARK. *Introduction to Poetry.* New York: Sloane, 1951. Brilliant brief analysis of "To . . . Wars."

WALL, L. N. "Some Notes on Marvell's Sources." *Notes and Queries,* CCII (1957), 70–73. Discusses Lovelace's influence on Marvell and lists parallels.

WALTON, GEOFFREY. "The Cavalier Poets." *From Donne to Marvell.* Ed. Boris Ford. London: Penguin Books, 1956. Good appraisal of Lovelace's sensibility.

WEDGWOOD, C. V. "Cavalier Poetry and Cavalier Politics." *Velvet Studies.* London: J. Cape, 1946. Fine evocation of Cavalier and court milieux.

Index